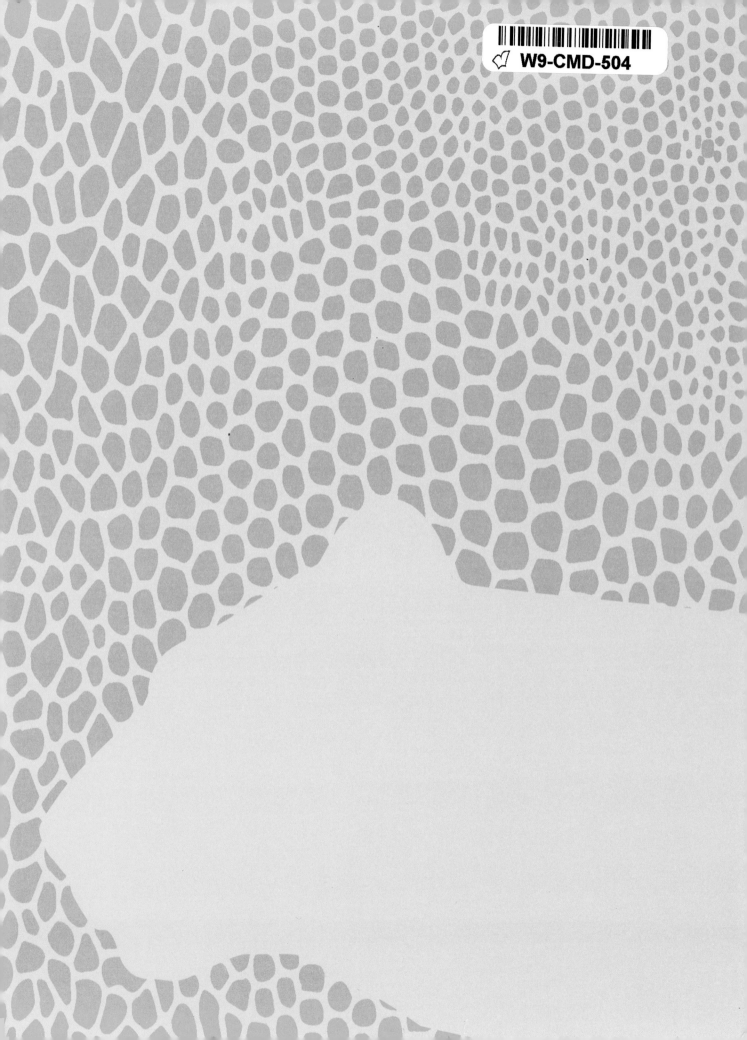

ANIMAL
KNOWLEDGE
GENIUS!

DK Delhi

Senior Editor Rupa Rao
Senior Art Editor Vikas Chauhan
Editorial Team Nandini Tripathy, Janashree Singha, Hina Jain
Art Editors Tanisha Mandal, Noopur Dalal,
Amisha Gupta, Devika Awasthi
Jacket Designer Juhi Sheth
Senior DTP Designer Vishal Bhatia
DTP Designers Vijay Kandwal, Rakesh Kumar
Project Picture Researcher Deepak Negi
Managing Jackets Editor Saloni Singh
Pre-Production Manager Balwant Singh
Production Manager Pankaj Sharma
Picture Research Manager Taiyaba Khatoon
Managing Editor Soma B. Chowdhury
Managing Art Editor Govind Mittal
Editorial Head Glenda Fernandes
Design Head Malavika Talukder

DK London

Senior Editor Ashwin Khurana
Senior Designer Rachael Grady
US Editor Megan Douglass
US Executive Editor Lori Cates Hand
Jacket Designer Akiko Kato
Jacket Design Development Manager Sophia MTT
Production Editor Kavita Varma
Production Controller Sian Cheung
Managing Editor Francesca Baines
Managing Art Editor Philip Letsu
Publisher Andrew Macintyre
Associate Publishing Director Liz Wheeler
Art Director Karen Self
Publishing Director Jonathan Metcalf

First American Edition, 2021
Published in the United States by DK Publishing
1450 Broadway, Suite 801, New York, NY 10018

A catalog record for this book
is available from the Library of Congress.
ISBN 978-0-7440-3959-7

DK books are available at special discounts when purchased
in bulk for sales promotions, premiums, fund-raising, or educational use.
For details, contact: DK Publishing Special Markets, 1450 Broadway,
Suite 801, New York, NY 10018
SpecialSales@dk.com

Printed and bound in China

For the curious
www.dk.com

MIX
Paper from
responsible sources
FSC™ C018179

This book was made with Forest Stewardship
Council™ certified paper—one small step
in DK's commitment to a sustainable future.
For more information go to
www.dk.com/our-green-pledge

ANIMAL
KNOWLEDGE
GENIUS!

Written by: Stevie Derrick and Lizzie Munsey
Consultant: John Woodward

DK

CONTENTS

How this book works

Welcome to this fact-packed, quiz-filled challenge. Top up with some new knowledge and then put your brain to the test by matching the picture clues with the answers. Can you tell a coral from a jellyfish? Do you know which beak belongs to which bird? Can you identify your lizards? It is time to find out!

01. There are seven chapters all about animals—their similarities, differences, and lives on Earth—and lots of quizzes. Perhaps start with one that you know all about, and then move on to something new.

Facts first

First read up on the main groups that make up the animal kingdom: invertebrates, fish, amphibians, reptiles, birds, and mammals. Filled with essential information, these pages will warm up your brain for the quizzes.

Next the challenge

Then it's time to test yourself. Take a look at the pictures and the list of answers in the panel on the side and try to match them up. Follow these four steps for the best way to tackle things.

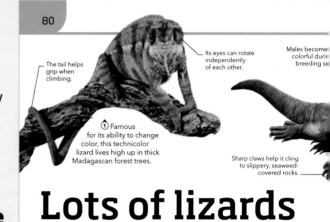

80

The tail helps grip when climbing.

Its eyes can rotate independently of each other.

Males become colorful durin breeding se

① Famous for its ability to change color, this technicolor lizard lives high up in thick Madagascan forest trees.

Sharp claws help it cling to slippery, seaweed-covered rocks.

Lots of lizards

Forming the biggest group of reptiles, with more than 5,500 species, lizards come in all shapes and sizes—from tiny geckos to the 10-ft- (3-m-) long Komodo dragon. These scaly, cold-blooded animals are found on every continent except Antarctica.

Black st across t

Sti its sm

④ When threatened, this creature puffs up its body to make itself look bigger, while also sticking out its tongue and hissing.

Fold neck body

The long tail s up two-thirds ts body length.

cko 4. Blue-tongued skink 5. Green iguana 10. Thorny devil 11. Frilled lizard

---

66 AMPHIBIANS

Amphibians

This group of animals can all breathe through their skin, which has to be kept moist at all times to absorb oxygen. As a result most amphibians live their whole lives in damp places. Some may also use organs called gills to breathe underwater, while others can develop lungs, which let them breathe air on land.

How to swim like a frog

01. Use your front legs and feet to make small movements, steering and controlling the direction of your body.

Suckers on the toes help the frog grip when on land.

Frogs cannot survive in salt water.

Tiny ponds
Some frogs carry their tadpoles on their backs to release them into pools of water collected by plants high in rainforest trees.

02. Stretch out as far as possible, then pull your front legs down to your sides.

03. Kick hard with your powerful hind legs and use your webbed feet to push forward.

Gills are organs used to take in oxygen from the water.

Adult

Egg

Larva with four limbs

Larva with gill buds

Larva with two limbs

Salamander life cycle

Over its life, a salamander's body undergoes significant changes. It starts as an egg. The egg hatches into a larva in 19-50 days, which slowly develops gills, eventually becoming an adult in 2-5 months.

Vocal sac inflates during croaking.

Webbed toes help the frog push through the water.

Croaking

Male frogs and toads croak to attract females, and the louder they croak the more likely they are to succeed in finding a mate. Each species of frog and toad has its own unique croak.

Deadly defenses

⚠ Found only in Colombia, the golden poison-dart frog is one of the most toxic animals on Earth. It stores its poison in its skin.

⚠ The tiny phantasmal poison frog only grows up to 1½ in (4 cm) in length, but still carries enough poison to kill a human.

⚠ Just touching the skin of the red-headed poison frog (below) would be enough to make you violently ill.

I don't believe it

The tadpole of the South American paradoxical frog is three times the size of the adult frog. It can be up to 10in (25cm) long, shrinking as it gets older.

Types of amphibians

Frogs and toads
This is the biggest amphibian group. These creatures have long, strong back legs and shorter front legs.

Newts and salamanders
These amphibians have lizard-like bodies, with long tails and four even-size limbs.

Caecilians
Wormlike and limbless, these amphibians are rarely seen. They live underground or underwater.

In numbers

60
The number of days a male Darwin's frog keeps tadpoles in his vocal sac after hatching. He then coughs up tiny frogs.

15 mph
(24 km/h) The maximum speed of the Andean salamander, the world's fastest amphibian.

6½ lb
(3kg) The weight of a single adult goliath frog.

Biggest and smallest

6ft (1.8m)

6ft (1.8m)
The biggest of all amphibians is the colossal Chinese giant salamander. It lives in streams and rivers in central China.

⅞ in (18mm) diameter

The tiniest amphibian is a frog, Paedophryne amauensis, from Papua New Guinea. Shown here on a US dime, it is ¼ in (7mm) long.

67

No peeking
You'll find the answers matched with the numbers of the correct pictures at the bottom of the page.

02. When you have chosen a quiz, take a careful look at the pictures. Can you identify all the animals? The clues will give you extra information to help you work things out.

03. Look at the "Test Yourself" panel and match the words and pictures. Don't write the answers in the book—you may want to quiz again later to improve your score, or give it to a friend to see how they do.

lives on rocky shores of s Islands, where it feeds ome even dive down to the bottom of the sea.

y the strongest males small species are right blue in color. Females, the young, and weaker males are green or brown.

⑥ The biggest lizard of all, this huge reptile is found only on a few small islands in Indonesia. Sailors once mistook it for a mythical beast.

The forked tongue is flicked out and can detect food from as far as 3 miles (5 km) away.

⑦ This flame-red creature is shier than its colors suggest. It spends much of its time hiding in burrows.

The tail can detach when a predator attacks.

⑧ This venomous North American lizard has a fearsome reputation of crushing its prey to death.

"Armored" skin with small, strong scales

⑨ Found only in the rainforests of a large East African island, this lizard can drink nectar from flowers.

Sharp claws on its feet help dig burrows.

Large, strong toe pads for grip

The tail is held upright when walking.

⑩ Small and spiky, this creature lives in dry desert areas in central Australia.

⑪ This vibrant reptile lives in North America. It can change color, but is not a chameleon.

The pink throat pouch is used to attract mates.

Fan of skin opens up when the lizard opens its mouth wide.

⑫ If a flash of its wide neck ruff is not enough to put off a predator, this lizard makes a run for it, sometimes rising up on to two legs.

ANSWERS: 1. Panther chameleon 6. Komodo dragon 7. Fire skink 8.

TEST YOURSELF

STARTER	CHALLENGER	GENIUS!
Panther chameleon	**Marine iguana**	**Madagascar day gecko**
Green iguana	**Frilled lizard**	**Green anole**
Blue-tongued skink	**Thorny devil**	**Fire skink**
Turquoise dwarf gecko	**Komodo dragon**	**Gila monster**

04. Work your way through the three levels of difficulty—it's not supposed to be easy! When you think you've got them all, check the answers—they are upside down at the bottom of the page.

Start off easy ... These answers should be the easiest to figure out.

Getting harder ... How about these harder answers? Can you match them, too?

Truly tricky If you can figure out these final answers it's official—you're a genius!

1

THE ANIMAL WORLD

Life all around us

Our world is full of amazing animals adapted to every habitat, from scorching hot deserts to tropical rainforests. There is an incredible diversity of life in water, too, lurking in freshwater rivers and lakes, sunlit coral reefs, and deep, dark ocean trenches.

Types of animals

Invertebrates

Making up 97 percent of the animal kingdom, invertebrates are the only group that do not have an internal skeleton. From marine sponges to spiders, there is an extraordinary variety of species.

Fish

All fish live in water, from freshwater lakes to deep ocean trenches. They breathe under water using their gills, and their bodies are covered in scales, which are tiny plates made of thin bone.

Amphibians
These cold-blooded creatures with wet skin can breathe on land as well as in water. Most of them lay eggs, which typically develop into tadpoles before taking on their adult form.

Reptiles

These animals are cold-blooded—they cannot control their body temperature and rely on heat from the sun to warm them up. Their bodies are covered in scales.

Birds

The only animals to have feathers, birds use them to fly and keep themselves warm. Birds are warm-blooded, and also have beaks, which they use for hunting and eating.

Mammals

All mammals are warm-blooded—they generate heat inside their body and can control their body temperature. All mammals have hair or fur on their bodies. When first born, young are raised on milk from their mothers.

What is an animal?

Animals are living things that can eat, move, breathe, communicate, sense the world, and give birth to more beings like themselves. Scientists think there are up to eight million species of animals worldwide—but a vast majority have yet to be discovered!

How to move like a jellyfish

01. As an animal, you have the ability to move, to feed, and protect yourself from predators. Relax the muscles in your bell to draw water into your body.

New life
All animals reproduce. Some of them lay eggs, while others give birth to live young. This newly hatched baby turtle is making its way to the sea.

In numbers

90%
Estimated number of plant and animal species that are still unknown.

600 million
The number of years animals have existed on Earth.

322
Number of animal species that went extinct in the last 500 years.

I don't believe it

Humans share 98.8 percent of chimpanzee DNA. Even so, there are 35 million differences between the two species.

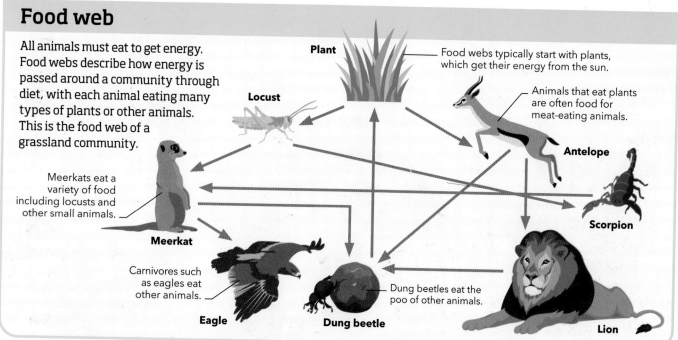

All animals need oxygen to survive. Most animals that live on land or fly breathe it in from the air using their lungs or air tubes.

Some water-dwelling animals use organs called gills to absorb oxygen from water.

Mosquito larvae live in water but breathe in oxygen from the air using a tube attached to breathing holes in their tails.

Lungless salamanders absorb oxygen through membranes in their mouth, throat, and skin.

Most snakes have only one working lung—an adaptation to their slender, tubelike bodies.

03. You can travel up to 0.6 mile (1 km) each day as you feed on plankton.

02. Contract your muscles to push the water back out, which will propel you forward.

Food web

All animals must eat to get energy. Food webs describe how energy is passed around a community through diet, with each animal eating many types of plants or other animals. This is the food web of a grassland community.

Plant

Food webs typically start with plants, which get their energy from the sun.

Locust

Animals that eat plants are often food for meat-eating animals.

Antelope

Meerkats eat a variety of food including locusts and other small animals.

Scorpion

Meerkat

Carnivores such as eagles eat other animals.

Dung beetles eat the poo of other animals.

Eagle

Dung beetle

Lion

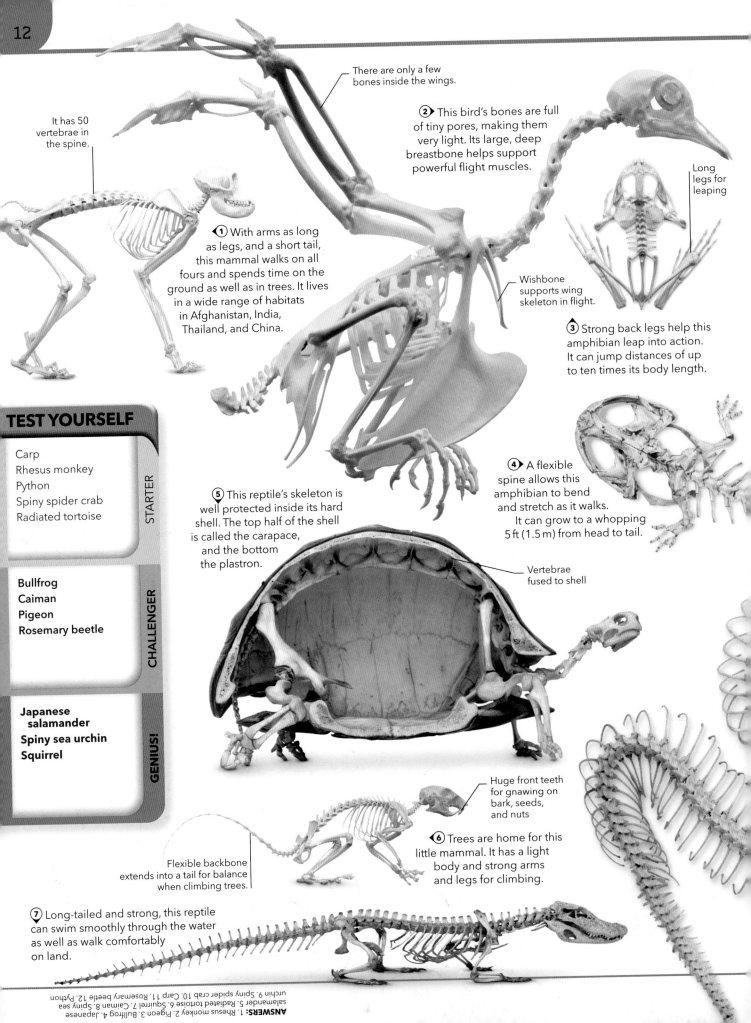

It has 50 vertebrae in the spine.

There are only a few bones inside the wings.

② This bird's bones are full of tiny pores, making them very light. Its large, deep breastbone helps support powerful flight muscles.

Long legs for leaping

① With arms as long as legs, and a short tail, this mammal walks on all fours and spends time on the ground as well as in trees. It lives in a wide range of habitats in Afghanistan, India, Thailand, and China.

Wishbone supports wing skeleton in flight.

③ Strong back legs help this amphibian leap into action. It can jump distances of up to ten times its body length.

④ A flexible spine allows this amphibian to bend and stretch as it walks. It can grow to a whopping 5 ft (1.5 m) from head to tail.

⑤ This reptile's skeleton is well protected inside its hard shell. The top half of the shell is called the carapace, and the bottom the plastron.

Vertebrae fused to shell

TEST YOURSELF

STARTER

Carp
Rhesus monkey
Python
Spiny spider crab
Radiated tortoise

CHALLENGER

Bullfrog
Caiman
Pigeon
Rosemary beetle

GENIUS!

Japanese salamander
Spiny sea urchin
Squirrel

Flexible backbone extends into a tail for balance when climbing trees.

Huge front teeth for gnawing on bark, seeds, and nuts

⑥ Trees are home for this little mammal. It has a light body and strong arms and legs for climbing.

⑦ Long-tailed and strong, this reptile can swim smoothly through the water as well as walk comfortably on land.

Bare bones

Most animals have a skeleton—a framework that shapes bodies and helps anchor muscles. Animals with internal skeletons and backbones are called vertebrates. Creatures without backbones are known as invertebrates, although some of these animals have an armor-like casing, called an exoskeleton.

Legs are rigid tubes with flexible joints

9 A spiky body and long, thin legs are features of this animal's exoskeleton. It lives in water, and algae often grow on top of its rough shell—excellent for camouflage.

8 This marine invertebrate has a skeleton made of plates that are covered with a layer of skin. It feeds on algae, small animals, and decaying matter.

Fins are not attached to the backbone.

Bony plates protect the head.

10 Perfect for life in the water, this streamlined skeleton lets its owner swim smoothly with just a flip of the fins.

Short ribs

11 This creature has a shiny purple-and-green striped exoskeleton. It enjoys munching on herbs, much to the dismay of gardeners.

Long, very flexible backbone with hundreds of curved ribs

12 This reptile lacks limbs but has a very long backbone, which is ideal for slithering along when searching for prey.

Deforestation
When forests are cut down, the habitats of a wide range of animals are destroyed. This fire has been started to clear a rainforest for farming land.

Climate change
Human activity has warmed our planet. As Earth heats up, the ice caps melt, reducing the areas where animals such as penguins live.

Poaching and the pet trade
Although against the law, some animals, such as elephants, are killed for their body parts. Others, like macaws, are sold illegally as pets.

Construction
Dams provide cheap, renewable electricity. However, building them can flood valleys and block rivers, depriving or killing the animals, especially fish, there.

Under threat

Humans have changed the world around us. We farm the land, fish the oceans, and pollute the air with our cars and factories. This has had a negative impact on the natural world, with habitats destroyed and the survival of the animals that live in them threatened. For some species it is already too late—they have become extinct.

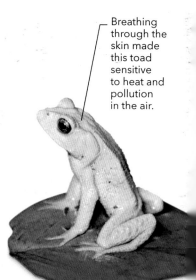

Breathing through the skin made this toad sensitive to heat and pollution in the air.

Species in danger

The International Union for Conservation of Nature (IUCN) has calculated the approximate percentage (shown below in red) of the five vertebrate animal types under threat. There are no similar measurements for invertebrates, but experts know they face a crisis.

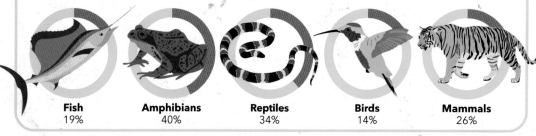

Fish	Amphibians	Reptiles	Birds	Mammals
19%	40%	34%	14%	26%

Gone forever

Golden toads lived in a small area of the rainforest in Costa Rica. When a change in climate made the area hotter and drier, the population fell sick with a fungal disease. By 1989, only one was found. Today, they are extinct.

Biodiversity hot spots

Some places on Earth have a variety of plants and animals that are not found elsewhere. Where these areas are under threat, they are known as biodiversity hot spots. Across the world, 36 biodiversity hot spots have been identified. They cover just 2.4 percent of Earth's land surface but more than 50 percent of plant species and 43 percent of bird, mammal, amphibian, and reptile species are found only in these areas.

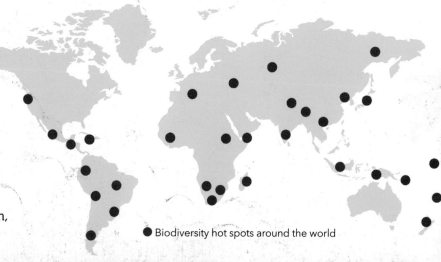

● Biodiversity hot spots around the world

Overfishing
Over time, humans have taken so many fish out of the oceans that many are now scarce. Some, like the smooth handfish, from Australia, have become extinct.

Disease and pesticides
Spraying pesticides kills insects that eat crops. But this upsets the fragile ecosystem as birds lose a source of food, and may be poisoned in turn.

I don't believe it

Humans have been driving animals to extinction for thousands of years. It is likely that hunting contributed to the extinction of megafauna (huge animals), such as woolly mammoths, more than 10,000 years ago.

Near extinction

The world's most endangered marine mammal is the vaquita, a small porpoise found only in the Gulf of California. Some conservationists estimate that there may be fewer than 10 vaquitas left in the wild.

How the Sumatran rhinoceros has become critically endangered

01. Vast areas of tropical forest where the world's smallest rhino lives have been lost to logging. Rhino numbers have declined by 70 percent over the last 20 years.

02. This deforestation has split up rhino populations, making it difficult for them to find a mate and breed.

There are fewer than 80 Sumatran rhinos left in the wild.

03. The Sumatran rhino is also threatened by poachers, who hunt it for its two horns.

The International Union for Conservation of Nature (IUCN) Red List shows which animals are at risk of extinction. It puts each animal into one of these categories.

Least concern
These animals have stable populations. For now, they are unlikely to become extinct.

Near threatened
Not currently threatened, but may become so in the near future.

Vulnerable
Populations are threatened. These animals face a high risk of extinction in the wild.

Endangered
These animals face a very high risk of becoming extinct in the wild.

Critically endangered
Few animals remain, they face an extremely high, immediate extinction risk.

Conservation

Working to protect habitats and the plants and animals that live in them is known as conservation. Setting up wildlife reserves and national parks, and laws against poaching, can be an effective way of doing this, as it protects whole ecosystems (all living and nonliving things in an area), especially animals that are in danger of becoming extinct.

How to protect an orphaned elephant

263 orphaned elephants have been rescued as part of a rehabilitation program.

01. Set up a wildlife reserve in an area where there are young elephants that need your protection. The reserve shown here is in Kenya in Africa.

Extinct in the wild
These animals no longer exist in the wild, only in captivity, such as in zoos.

Extinct
No living members survive, or the last individuals are of the same sex, so cannot reproduce.

Tag attached to shell

Keeping track
Scientists learn about endangered hawksbill turtles by tracking their movements, using satellite tags.

1,000,000
The estimated number of species currently at risk of extinction.

64,500 sq ft
(6,000 sq m) The area of forest that is cut down every second.

99%
The percentage of currently threatened species that are at risk due to human activities.

40%
The percentage of insect species that could go extinct in less than a century due to habitat loss.

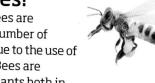

Save the bees!
Across the world, bees are disappearing for a number of reasons, but mainly due to the use of pesticides that kill them. Bees are essential for the pollination of plants both in nature and in agriculture, particularly for fruit and vegetable farming. You can help bees by not using pesticides, and by planting flowers full of delicious nectar for them to collect.

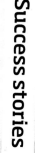

I don't believe it
There are 100,000 wildlife reserves and national parks around the world today. They offer much-needed protection to animals, plants, and their habitats. They also allow humans to experience the wilderness.

02. Hire rangers to patrol the area and guard the elephants from poachers and hunters. They may also need to feed and care for any particularly vulnerable animals, such as baby elephants orphaned when their mothers were killed by poachers.

03. Encourage sustainable tourism, which has a minimal impact on the environment and helps create jobs for local people, so you can raise funds to continue your conservation project.

🏆 There were only four Mauritius kestrels left in the wild by the early 1970s. After a captive breeding program, there are now hundreds.

🏆 Recent conservation work has increased the number of mountain gorillas from around 600 to more than 1,000.

🏆 The California condor was hunted to near extinction, but captive-bred birds have now been released back into the wild.

2

INVERTEBRATES

Huddle together

Most types of animals on Earth are invertebrates. They include insects such as these ladybugs, which have clumped together in thousands in a sheltered place to sleep through the cold winter, when there is nothing for them to eat.

Invertebrates

Animals without an internal, jointed skeleton are known as invertebrates. These were the first creatures to evolve on our planet, and are incredibly varied. From insects on land to octopuses in the sea, invertebrates make up 97 percent of all animals on Earth.

Types of invertebrates

There are 34 main groups of invertebrates, six of which are shown here.

Coelenterates
This group includes comb jellies, corals, sea anemones, and jellyfish. Most have stinging tentacles that they use to catch prey.

Sponges
These simple creatures live all of their lives attached to a solid surface such as a rock in lakes, rivers, and oceans.

Echinoderms
With spiny skins, these invertebrates live in water. Some have a starlike appearance, while others look like cucumbers.

Mollusks
These soft-bodied animals include snails and slugs, octopuses, squids, and oysters. Some have shells, while others do not.

Arthropods
This is the largest group of invertebrates, and is mostly made up of insects, but also includes crabs and spiders.

Worms
With soft, segmented bodies, these animals include earthworms as well as many colorful marine species.

MAGIC ARMS
A starfish can grow a new arm if it loses one. It can even regrow a new body from an arm, as seen above. This is because each arm contains a full set of vital organs.

I don't believe it
Although only ⅜ in (1 cm) long, the Antarctic midge insect is the largest land animal native to Antarctica.

Master of disguise

The intelligent mimic octopus has perfected the art of disguise. To hide from predators, this marine invertebrate can change its color and texture to look like rocks, coral, and even other animals.

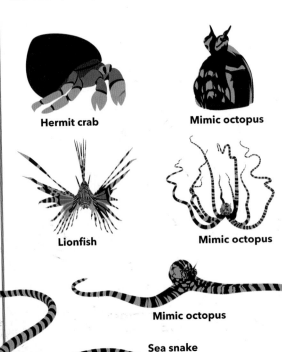

Hermit crab

Mimic octopus

Lionfish

Mimic octopus

Mimic octopus

Sea snake

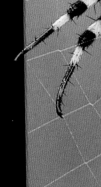

How to hunt like a spider

01. Spin a web made from strong, stretchy silk threads to trap flying insects.

02. Wait patiently until you sense from the vibrations that an insect has become stuck. Quickly scuttle over.

03. Inject the insect with special digestive juices that will liquefy its insides. Suck up the liquid and enjoy the feast!

In numbers

300 million
The number of years that dragonflies have existed on Earth. They were some of the first winged insects to evolve.

550 lb
(250 kg) The maximum recorded weight of a giant clam—the largest mollusk in the world.

24
The number of eyes a box jellyfish has, to help it avoid obstacles.

Life cycle of a jellyfish

Jellyfish hatch as drifting larvae, which then become tiny life-forms called polyps that cling to rocks. Each polyp eventually forms segments, which separate into individual jellyfish that grow into adults. Depending on the species, the process can take from several weeks to months.

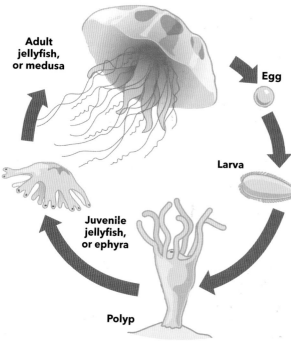

Adult jellyfish, or medusa

Egg

Larva

Juvenile jellyfish, or ephyra

Polyp

Glowing in the dark

✦ Scorpions have a special mineral in their skin that shines a blue-green color when under ultraviolet light. Some scientists believe that it could be for protection against parasitic ticks and mites.

✦ Comb jellies produce light flashes to startle predators.

✦ Despite their name, fireflies are actually flying beetles. A chemical reaction in their bodies allows them to light up. They use the glow to communicate with other fireflies.

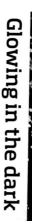

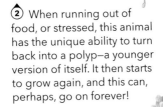

① With hairlike tentacles that can grow up to 120 ft (36.5 m) long, this invertebrate feeds on ragworms, fish, and other small aquatic animals.

② When running out of food, or stressed, this animal has the unique ability to turn back into a polyp—a younger version of itself. It then starts to grow again, and this can, perhaps, go on forever!

Fingerlike tentacles can contract if the animal feels threatened.

Corals and jellies

These aquatic animals are some of the simplest life-forms on the planet and include cnidarians—jellyfish, corals, and anemones—comb jellies, and sponges. They have been around for nearly 600 million years and are still thriving. Cnidarians are armed with stinging tentacles to paralyze their prey, while comb jellies and sponges feed by drawing water into their body to catch tiny organisms.

③ Living in tropical coral reefs, this grand-looking invertebrate attaches itself to rocks on the seabed. It uses its venomous tentacles to catch fish and small organisms drifting in the water.

④ This marine creature gets its name from the bulblike tips on its tentacles. Clownfish and other animals often live between the tentacles as they provide a refuge from predators.

⑤ This cnidarian may look like a plant, with bright branches that spread outward, but it is in fact a colony of tiny animals. It grows very slowly—about ½ in (1 cm) every year.

Tubelike structures can grow 3 ft (1 m) long.

⑥ Growing on shallow reefs, this creature feeds on bacteria and other tiny organisms that float through its hollow, cylinder-shaped branches.

⑧ Named after a serpent in Greek mythology, this tiny invertebrate grows up to just ¾ in (2 cm) long. It uses its stinging tentacles to stun, entangle, or kill its prey, and feasts on small freshwater organisms.

⑦ Found in rivers and lakes, this invertebrate is covered in tiny pores that filter the water around it for food. Its green coloring comes from the algae living on its body.

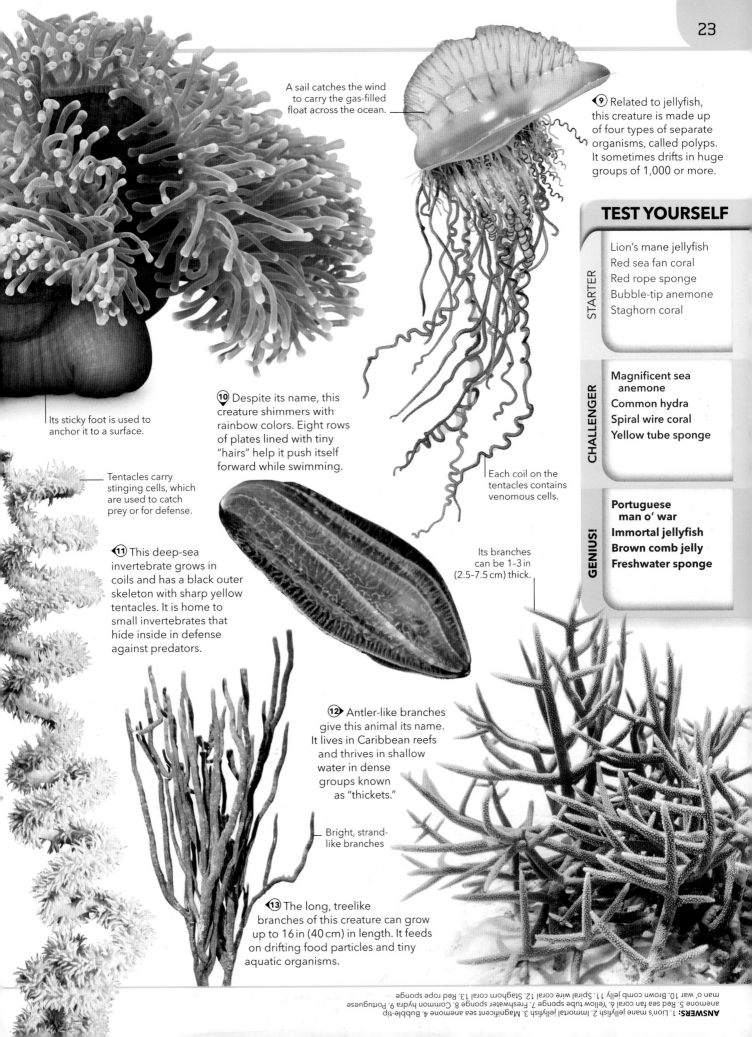

A sail catches the wind to carry the gas-filled float across the ocean.

9 Related to jellyfish, this creature is made up of four types of separate organisms, called polyps. It sometimes drifts in huge groups of 1,000 or more.

Its sticky foot is used to anchor it to a surface.

Tentacles carry stinging cells, which are used to catch prey or for defense.

10 Despite its name, this creature shimmers with rainbow colors. Eight rows of plates lined with tiny "hairs" help it push itself forward while swimming.

11 This deep-sea invertebrate grows in coils and has a black outer skeleton with sharp yellow tentacles. It is home to small invertebrates that hide inside in defense against predators.

Each coil on the tentacles contains venomous cells.

Its branches can be 1–3 in (2.5–7.5 cm) thick.

12 Antler-like branches give this animal its name. It lives in Caribbean reefs and thrives in shallow water in dense groups known as "thickets."

Bright, strand-like branches

13 The long, treelike branches of this creature can grow up to 16 in (40 cm) in length. It feeds on drifting food particles and tiny aquatic organisms.

TEST YOURSELF

STARTER
Lion's mane jellyfish
Red sea fan coral
Red rope sponge
Bubble-tip anemone
Staghorn coral

CHALLENGER
Magnificent sea anemone
Common hydra
Spiral wire coral
Yellow tube sponge

GENIUS!
Portuguese man o' war
Immortal jellyfish
Brown comb jelly
Freshwater sponge

Wiggly worms

Worms are soft creatures with long bodies. Some have many short legs while others have no legs at all. A few can grow to be very long. The longest worm ever recorded is the bootlace worm, which can reach up to 180 ft (55 m) in length—longer than an Olympic-size swimming pool!

Thickened section of the body is used to store eggs.

1 By burrowing through the soil, this creature mixes it up and aerates (adds oxygen to) it, helping plants grow. It is a familiar sight in gardens.

2 Growing up to 13¾ in (35 cm) long, this cylindrical animal is the most common worm to cause an infection of the small intestine inside humans.

Tentacles can reach up to 12 in (30 cm) in length.

Red gill plumes absorb gases from the water.

3 Named after the colorful stripe running along the center of its body, this marine worm lives in some Southeast Asian coral reefs.

It can grow up to 10 ft (3 m) in length.

4 Long, noodle-like tentacles give this brightly colored creature its name. It uses them to find food while most of its body stays hidden in cracks on the seafloor.

Tentacles are used for breathing and feeding.

White body is made of a material called chitin, also found in crab shells.

5 This ocean worm has long, fanlike plumes that it uses to catch food particles. Its body is hidden inside a soft, flexible tube that is buried in the sand. It retreats into this tube when it senses danger.

6 Living next to hot springs on the ocean floor, this pipelike animal has colonies of bacteria living inside it. These make food that the worm can use to build its tissues and grow in size.

⑦ A bloodsucking worm, this creature latches on to a host animal to feed on its blood. It first secretes a fluid around the bite mark to stop the blood from clotting!

Flat, segmented body is covered in bristles.

Disk-shaped sucker helps it hold on to prey such as fish and birds.

⑨ Feasting on anemones and small crustaceans, this ferocious creature deters predators with bristles that snap off when touched and release a venom, which causes a burning sensation.

⑧ Tiny bumps all over its body give this worm its soft, fabric-like appearance. Its ringed antennae are highly sensitive and help it find prey in its forest habitat.

⑩ Named for its squashed appearance, this worm lives in the gut of animals. It can grow up to 30 ft (9 m) in length.

Rainbow-colored body

Sticky slime is released from the mouth to trap small spiders and termites.

⑪ This creature burrows in wet sand and mud, and likes to munch on seaweed and small organisms. Fleshy spikes along the sides of its body act as gills allowing it to breathe underwater.

Suckers on its head attach to its host.

Antennae stick out of the sand to detect prey.

⑫ This worm waits under sand on the seabed for small fish to swim by. Once it spots its prey, it shoots out to catch it. Its jaws are powerful enough to split the fish in two!

TEST YOURSELF

STARTER
Blue-lined flatworm
Giant roundworm
Common earthworm
Leech
Tapeworm

CHALLENGER
Bearded fireworm
Spaghetti worm
Giant tube worm
Giant feather duster worm

GENIUS!
Bobbit worm
Velvet worm
King ragworm

② Munching its way through the leaves, stems, and roots of plants, this mollusk is a common pest on vegetable patches.

The long tentacles are used to detect light.

③ Named after a fruit, this slug is one of the slowest creatures in the world—it has a top speed of 6½ in (16.5 cm) per minute.

Eggs take a few weeks to hatch.

Hornlike sensory organs are used to find food and avoid predators.

① Green plantlike projections give this sea creature its name. It grows up to only ¼ in (5 mm) long, and feeds on green algae.

④ One of the largest land mollusks in the world, this creature has a conical shell that can be up to 8 in (20 cm) long.

Conical, spiral shell

Mollusks

These creatures have soft bodies and no backbones. Some mollusks are bivalves (have two shells), and around 80 percent are gastropods—slugs, snails, and their relatives. Many have strong shells for protection, while others have bright colors to warn predators that they are poisonous. Some mollusks live on land, although most are marine animals.

⑤ Often found feeding on plants and flowers, this animal retreats into its coiled shell during dry weather.

Eyestalk can grow back if cut off.

⑥ A native of Central and South America, this mollusk is named after its long, thin eye stalks. It has gills as well as lungs, and comes to the surface of the water to breathe.

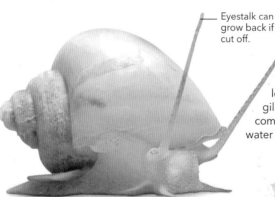

⑦ This bivalve has rectangular shells that look like the handle of a sharp blade. It buries itself in mud or sand, but has a siphon that sucks water into its mouth inside the shell.

⑧ This marine mollusk's antennae resemble a hopping mammal's ears. It uses them to detect chemicals in the water.

Horizontal ridges indicate growth and can be used to calculate its age.

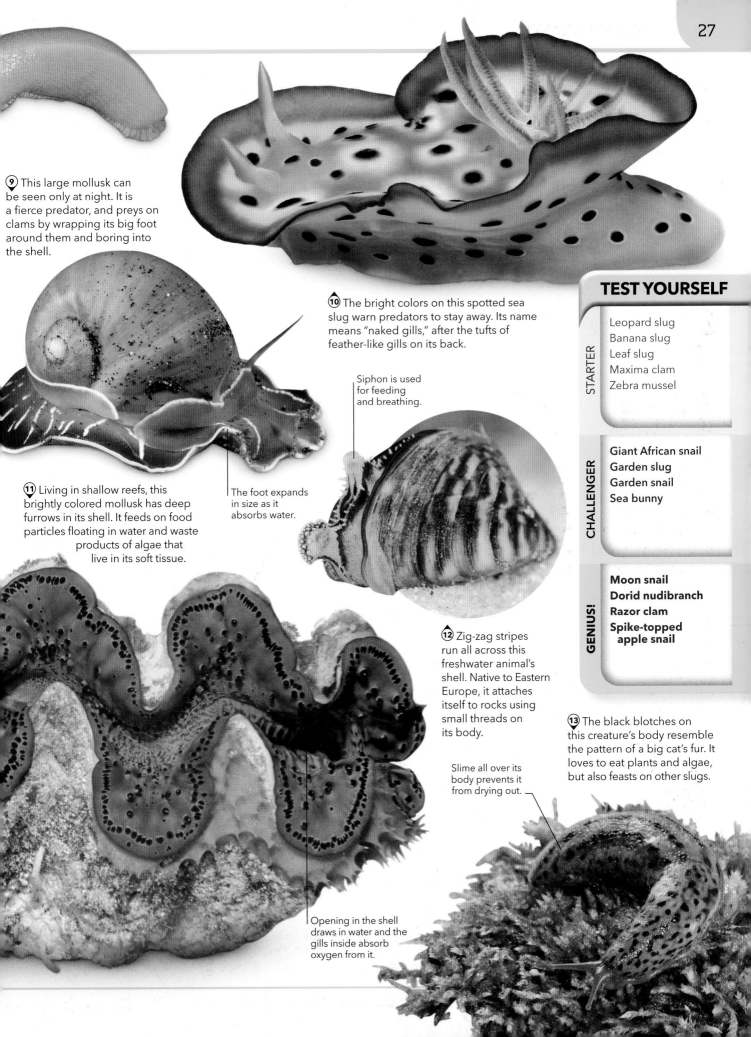

9 This large mollusk can be seen only at night. It is a fierce predator, and preys on clams by wrapping its big foot around them and boring into the shell.

10 The bright colors on this spotted sea slug warn predators to stay away. Its name means "naked gills," after the tufts of feather-like gills on its back.

Siphon is used for feeding and breathing.

11 Living in shallow reefs, this brightly colored mollusk has deep furrows in its shell. It feeds on food particles floating in water and waste products of algae that live in its soft tissue.

The foot expands in size as it absorbs water.

12 Zig-zag stripes run all across this freshwater animal's shell. Native to Eastern Europe, it attaches itself to rocks using small threads on its body.

Slime all over its body prevents it from drying out.

13 The black blotches on this creature's body resemble the pattern of a big cat's fur. It loves to eat plants and algae, but also feasts on other slugs.

Opening in the shell draws in water and the gills inside absorb oxygen from it.

TEST YOURSELF

STARTER
Leopard slug
Banana slug
Leaf slug
Maxima clam
Zebra mussel

CHALLENGER
Giant African snail
Garden slug
Garden snail
Sea bunny

GENIUS!
Moon snail
Dorid nudibranch
Razor clam
Spike-topped apple snail

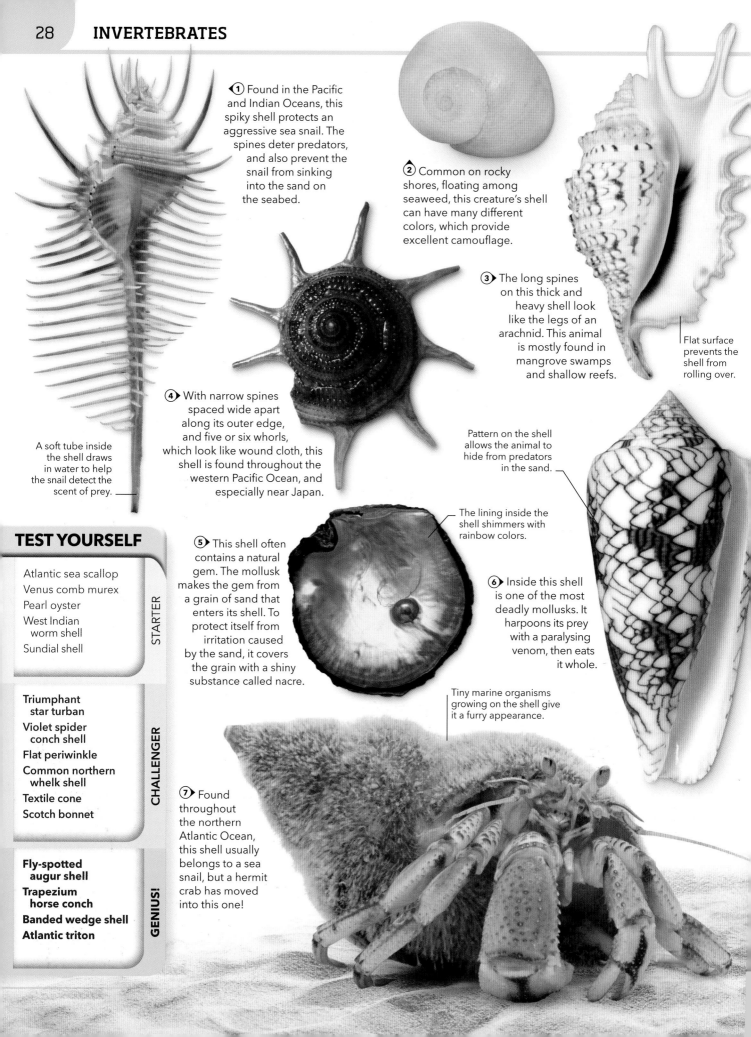

1 Found in the Pacific and Indian Oceans, this spiky shell protects an aggressive sea snail. The spines deter predators, and also prevent the snail from sinking into the sand on the seabed.

2 Common on rocky shores, floating among seaweed, this creature's shell can have many different colors, which provide excellent camouflage.

3 The long spines on this thick and heavy shell look like the legs of an arachnid. This animal is mostly found in mangrove swamps and shallow reefs.

Flat surface prevents the shell from rolling over.

4 With narrow spines spaced wide apart along its outer edge, and five or six whorls, which look like wound cloth, this shell is found throughout the western Pacific Ocean, and especially near Japan.

A soft tube inside the shell draws in water to help the snail detect the scent of prey.

Pattern on the shell allows the animal to hide from predators in the sand.

The lining inside the shell shimmers with rainbow colors.

5 This shell often contains a natural gem. The mollusk makes the gem from a grain of sand that enters its shell. To protect itself from irritation caused by the sand, it covers the grain with a shiny substance called nacre.

6 Inside this shell is one of the most deadly mollusks. It harpoons its prey with a paralysing venom, then eats it whole.

Tiny marine organisms growing on the shell give it a furry appearance.

7 Found throughout the northern Atlantic Ocean, this shell usually belongs to a sea snail, but a hermit crab has moved into this one!

TEST YOURSELF

STARTER

Atlantic sea scallop
Venus comb murex
Pearl oyster
West Indian worm shell
Sundial shell

CHALLENGER

Triumphant star turban
Violet spider conch shell
Flat periwinkle
Common northern whelk shell
Textile cone
Scotch bonnet

GENIUS!

Fly-spotted augur shell
Trapezium horse conch
Banded wedge shell
Atlantic triton

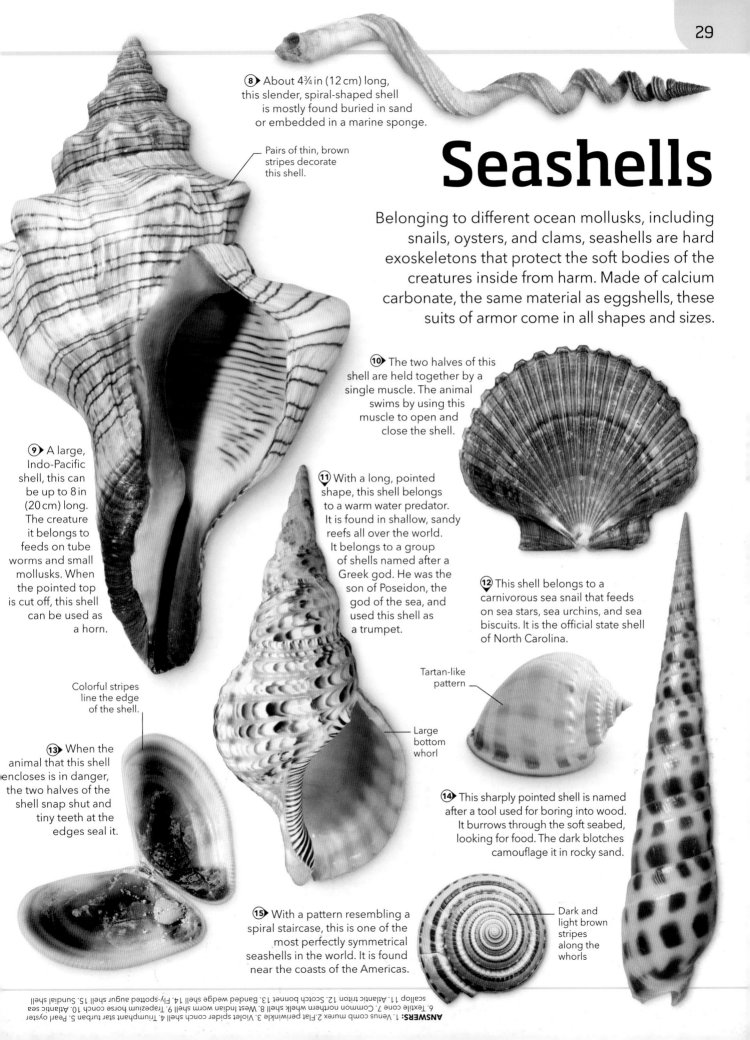

8 About 4¾ in (12 cm) long, this slender, spiral-shaped shell is mostly found buried in sand or embedded in a marine sponge.

Pairs of thin, brown stripes decorate this shell.

Seashells

Belonging to different ocean mollusks, including snails, oysters, and clams, seashells are hard exoskeletons that protect the soft bodies of the creatures inside from harm. Made of calcium carbonate, the same material as eggshells, these suits of armor come in all shapes and sizes.

10 The two halves of this shell are held together by a single muscle. The animal swims by using this muscle to open and close the shell.

9 A large, Indo-Pacific shell, this can be up to 8 in (20 cm) long. The creature it belongs to feeds on tube worms and small mollusks. When the pointed top is cut off, this shell can be used as a horn.

11 With a long, pointed shape, this shell belongs to a warm water predator. It is found in shallow, sandy reefs all over the world. It belongs to a group of shells named after a Greek god. He was the son of Poseidon, the god of the sea, and used this shell as a trumpet.

12 This shell belongs to a carnivorous sea snail that feeds on sea stars, sea urchins, and sea biscuits. It is the official state shell of North Carolina.

Tartan-like pattern

Colorful stripes line the edge of the shell.

13 When the animal that this shell encloses is in danger, the two halves of the shell snap shut and tiny teeth at the edges seal it.

Large bottom whorl

14 This sharply pointed shell is named after a tool used for boring into wood. It burrows through the soft seabed, looking for food. The dark blotches camouflage it in rocky sand.

15 With a pattern resembling a spiral staircase, this is one of the most perfectly symmetrical seashells in the world. It is found near the coasts of the Americas.

Dark and light brown stripes along the whorls

ANSWERS: 1. Venus comb murex 2. Flat periwinkle 3. Violet spider conch shell 4. Triumphant star turban 5. Pearl oyster 6. Textile cone 7. Common northern whelk 8. West Indian worm shell 9. Trapezium horse conch 10. Atlantic sea scallop 11. Atlantic triton 12. Scotch bonnet 13. Banded wedge shell 14. Fly-spotted augur shell 15. Sundial shell

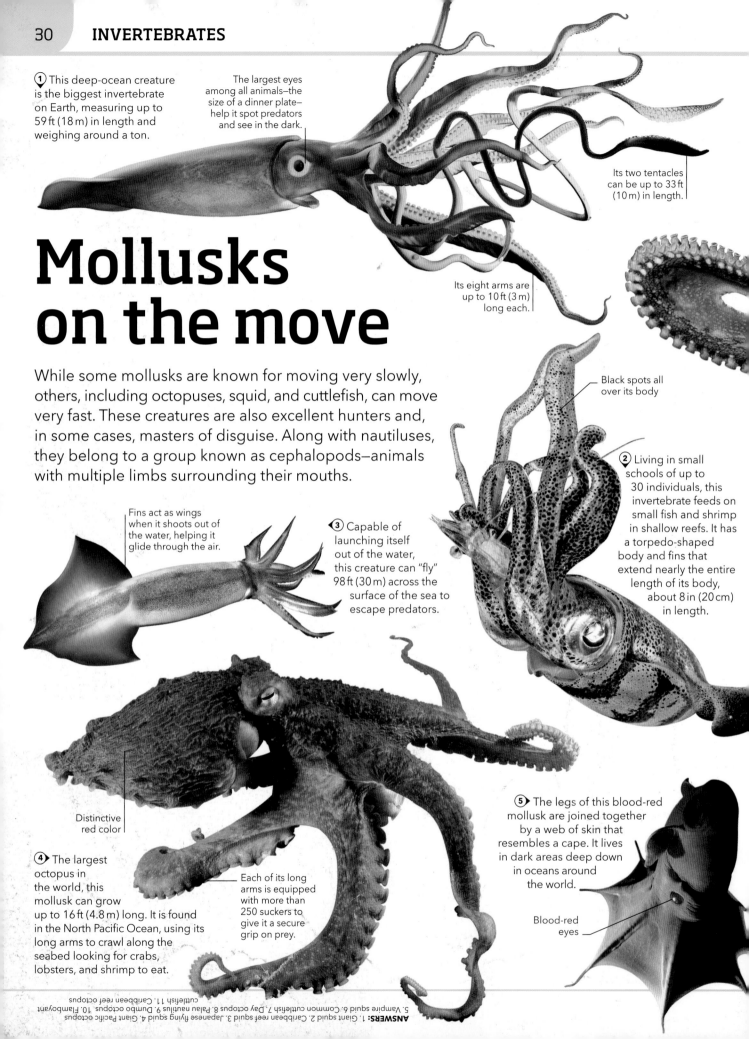

1 This deep-ocean creature is the biggest invertebrate on Earth, measuring up to 59 ft (18 m) in length and weighing around a ton.

The largest eyes among all animals—the size of a dinner plate—help it spot predators and see in the dark.

Its two tentacles can be up to 33 ft (10 m) in length.

Mollusks on the move

Its eight arms are up to 10 ft (3 m) long each.

While some mollusks are known for moving very slowly, others, including octopuses, squid, and cuttlefish, can move very fast. These creatures are also excellent hunters and, in some cases, masters of disguise. Along with nautiluses, they belong to a group known as cephalopods—animals with multiple limbs surrounding their mouths.

Black spots all over its body

2 Living in small schools of up to 30 individuals, this invertebrate feeds on small fish and shrimp in shallow reefs. It has a torpedo-shaped body and fins that extend nearly the entire length of its body, about 8 in (20 cm) in length.

Fins act as wings when it shoots out of the water, helping it glide through the air.

3 Capable of launching itself out of the water, this creature can "fly" 98 ft (30 m) across the surface of the sea to escape predators.

Distinctive red color

4 The largest octopus in the world, this mollusk can grow up to 16 ft (4.8 m) long. It is found in the North Pacific Ocean, using its long arms to crawl along the seabed looking for crabs, lobsters, and shrimp to eat.

Each of its long arms is equipped with more than 250 suckers to give it a secure grip on prey.

5 The legs of this blood-red mollusk are joined together by a web of skin that resembles a cape. It lives in dark areas deep down in oceans around the world.

Blood-red eyes

ANSWERS: 1. Giant squid 2. Caribbean reef squid 3. Japanese flying squid 4. Giant Pacific octopus 5. Vampire squid 6. Common cuttlefish 7. Day octopus 8. Palau nautilus 9. Dumbo octopus 10. Flamboyant cuttlefish 11. Caribbean reef octopus

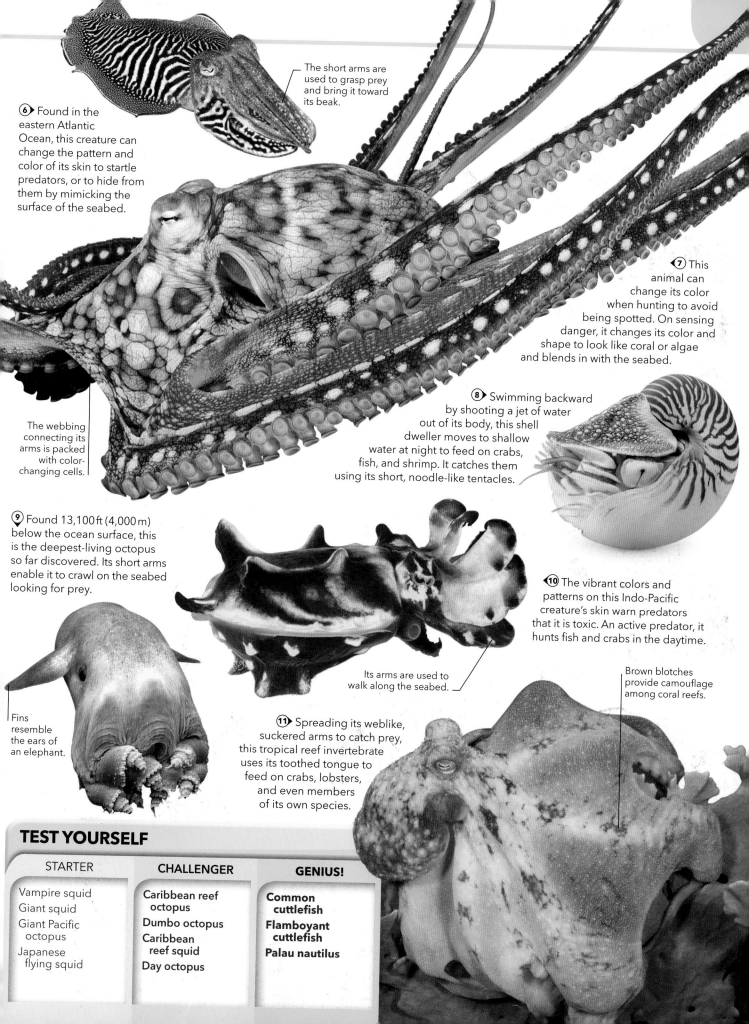

The short arms are used to grasp prey and bring it toward its beak.

6▶ Found in the eastern Atlantic Ocean, this creature can change the pattern and color of its skin to startle predators, or to hide from them by mimicking the surface of the seabed.

The webbing connecting its arms is packed with color-changing cells.

7▶ This animal can change its color when hunting to avoid being spotted. On sensing danger, it changes its color and shape to look like coral or algae and blends in with the seabed.

8▶ Swimming backward by shooting a jet of water out of its body, this shell dweller moves to shallow water at night to feed on crabs, fish, and shrimp. It catches them using its short, noodle-like tentacles.

9▶ Found 13,100 ft (4,000 m) below the ocean surface, this is the deepest-living octopus so far discovered. Its short arms enable it to crawl on the seabed looking for prey.

10▶ The vibrant colors and patterns on this Indo-Pacific creature's skin warn predators that it is toxic. An active predator, it hunts fish and crabs in the daytime.

Its arms are used to walk along the seabed.

Fins resemble the ears of an elephant.

Brown blotches provide camouflage among coral reefs.

11▶ Spreading its weblike, suckered arms to catch prey, this tropical reef invertebrate uses its toothed tongue to feed on crabs, lobsters, and even members of its own species.

TEST YOURSELF

STARTER	CHALLENGER	GENIUS!
Vampire squid	**Caribbean reef octopus**	**Common cuttlefish**
Giant squid	**Dumbo octopus**	**Flamboyant cuttlefish**
Giant Pacific octopus	**Caribbean reef squid**	**Palau nautilus**
Japanese flying squid	**Day octopus**	

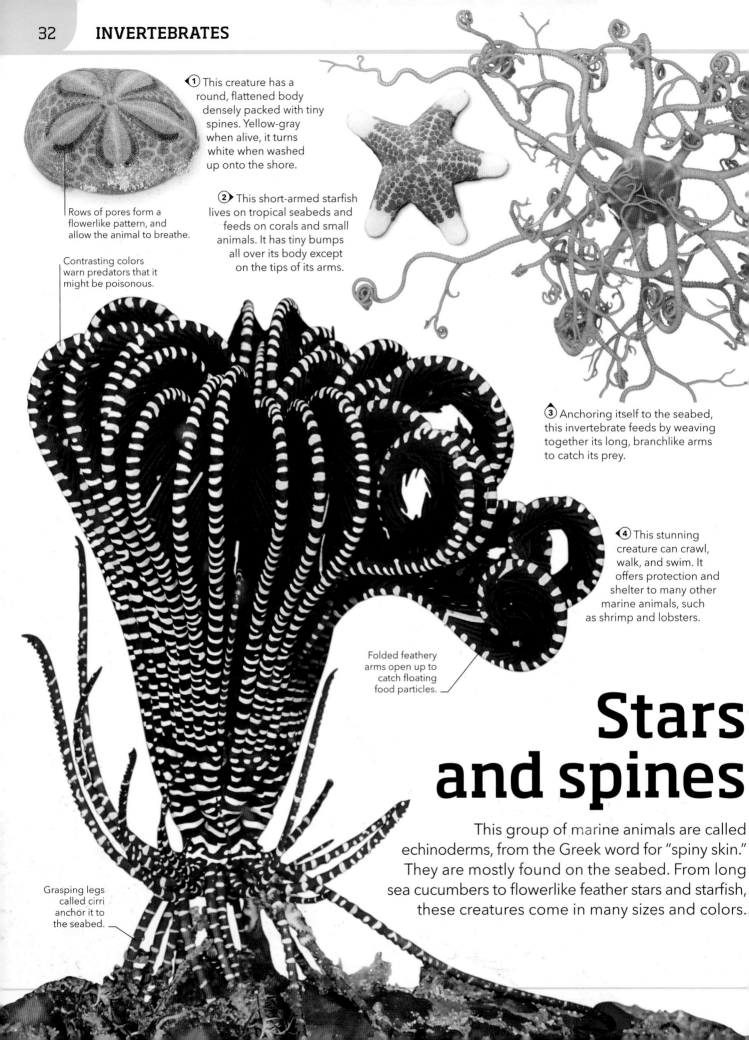

1 This creature has a round, flattened body densely packed with tiny spines. Yellow-gray when alive, it turns white when washed up onto the shore.

Rows of pores form a flowerlike pattern, and allow the animal to breathe.

Contrasting colors warn predators that it might be poisonous.

2 This short-armed starfish lives on tropical seabeds and feeds on corals and small animals. It has tiny bumps all over its body except on the tips of its arms.

3 Anchoring itself to the seabed, this invertebrate feeds by weaving together its long, branchlike arms to catch its prey.

4 This stunning creature can crawl, walk, and swim. It offers protection and shelter to many other marine animals, such as shrimp and lobsters.

Folded feathery arms open up to catch floating food particles.

Grasping legs called cirri anchor it to the seabed.

Stars and spines

This group of marine animals are called echinoderms, from the Greek word for "spiny skin." They are mostly found on the seabed. From long sea cucumbers to flowerlike feather stars and starfish, these creatures come in many sizes and colors.

The flexible arms can curl around themselves.

⑤ This knobbly Indo-Pacific species is mostly found among seaweed in shallow waters. It comes in colors ranging from light brown to deep orange.

Tubelike suckers on its legs help it move.

VIEW OF UNDERSIDE

The mouth is located on the underside.

Spiny bumps called tubercles on its upper side

VIEW FROM ABOVE

⑥ This is known to be the world's most venomous sea urchin. Its spines sting anything that may touch it, and the animal has few natural predators.

Petallike growths extend out of the spines and are used for feeding and cleaning.

⑦ This animal gets its name from its dark skin and long, rounded shape. When stressed, it secretes a sticky white substance, which can entangle predators.

Smooth, soft skin helps it slide through narrow spaces.

⑧ Hiding in dark crevices in the seabed by day, this creature emerges at night to feed on coral and algae. If threatened, it bristles its long spines.

Hard-tipped spines are venomous.

⑨ This animal gets its name from its golden brown body that is covered with dark brown blotches. It feeds on small particles off the seafloor.

Tube-like feet for moving across the seabed

⑩ Easily recognizable by the spikes covering its body, this creature is found on reefs in the Indian and Pacific Oceans. It feeds in large groups on hard corals.

It can have up to 21 spiny arms.

Five rows of sucker-like feet grip the rock and enable it to move.

⑪ This creature may grow up to 8 in (20 cm) long, but can swell to almost double its size by swallowing water when threatened.

TEST YOURSELF

STARTER
- Crown-of-thorns starfish
- Horned sea star
- Chocolate chip cucumber
- Long-spined sea urchin

CHALLENGER
- Flower urchin
- Black sea cucumber
- Sea apple cucumber
- Granulated sea star

GENIUS!
- Common basket star
- Elegant feather star
- Reticulated sea biscuit

ANSWERS: 1. Reticulated sea biscuit 2. Granulated sea star 3. Common basket star 4. Elegant feather star 5. Horned sea star 6. Flower urchin 7. Black sea cucumber 8. Long-spined sea urchin 9. Chocolate chip cucumber 10. Crown-of-thorns starfish 11. Sea apple cucumber

Armored animals

There are 40,000 species of crustaceans—animals with hard shells and jointed legs—on Earth. Most live underwater, but a few are land dwellers and prefer dark and damp spaces. How many can you recognize?

② Spanning 12½ ft (3.8 m) from claw to claw, and weighing 45 lb (20 kg), this is the world's largest crustacean. It is found in depths of 1,640 ft (500 m) below sea level.

Pincers that are capable of prying open mollusc shells.

① At just a few millimeters in length, this crustacean is one of the smallest. Its outer shell is almost transparent, so you can see its insides.

Grows up to 6 in (15 cm) in length.

Pouch can hold up to 20 eggs.

③ This stripy crustacean feeds on worms and other debris on the seafloor. It can produce as many as 800,000 eggs in a single spawning.

Long antennae allow it to sense its surroundings.

④ This little orange crustacean lives in self-dug burrows on the seafloor. It emerges at night to feed on other crustaceans, mollusks, worms, and starfish.

Eyes rotate independently to detect the prey's exact range for an accurate strike

⑤ This creature's club-like claws pack a powerful punch at 50 mph (80 km/h)—the fastest of any animal. It can smash its way through the shell of a crab, killing it instantly.

Hard, armor-like external skeleton

Feathery limbs to find food from the sea

⑥ Found stuck to rocks and boats, this relative of the shrimp grows a chalky shell to protect the soft body inside.

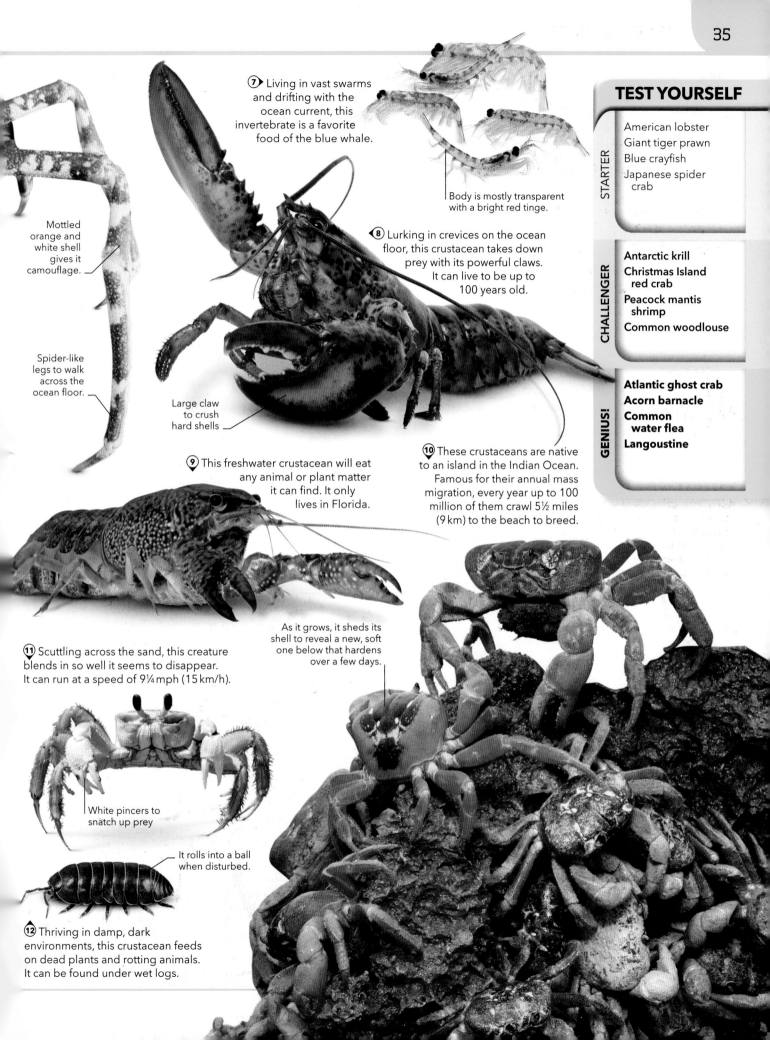

⑦ Living in vast swarms and drifting with the ocean current, this invertebrate is a favorite food of the blue whale.

Body is mostly transparent with a bright red tinge.

Mottled orange and white shell gives it camouflage.

⑧ Lurking in crevices on the ocean floor, this crustacean takes down prey with its powerful claws. It can live to be up to 100 years old.

Spider-like legs to walk across the ocean floor.

Large claw to crush hard shells

⑨ This freshwater crustacean will eat any animal or plant matter it can find. It only lives in Florida.

⑩ These crustaceans are native to an island in the Indian Ocean. Famous for their annual mass migration, every year up to 100 million of them crawl 5½ miles (9 km) to the beach to breed.

As it grows, it sheds its shell to reveal a new, soft one below that hardens over a few days.

⑪ Scuttling across the sand, this creature blends in so well it seems to disappear. It can run at a speed of 9¼ mph (15 km/h).

White pincers to snatch up prey

It rolls into a ball when disturbed.

⑫ Thriving in damp, dark environments, this crustacean feeds on dead plants and rotting animals. It can be found under wet logs.

① This tiny creature grows to only ¹⁄₁₀ in (4 mm) long. Males lift their colorful stomach flap like a fan to perform a courtship dance.

② Armed with venom that is 15 times stronger than that of a rattlesnake, females of this species are recognized by a red, hourglass-shaped marking on the stomach.

White-tipped, tufted legs

Red jaw is displayed when angry.

Front legs are raised to threaten enemies.

③ Extremely aggressive and venomous, this South American arachnid roams the forest floor at night, searching for prey.

④ The light color of this creature gives it excellent camouflage in its desert habitat. The stinger on its tail is mostly used for defense, but can also subdue its prey.

Small pincers are used to seize insects and spiders.

Arachnids

Specialized predators that can sting, bite, or rip apart their prey, arachnids have eight legs, two main body parts, and up to eight eyes. A few trap their prey by spinning large webs of silk, while others grab and crush theirs using strong claws.

Slender legs help it walk on water.

⑤ Hunting on the edges of ponds and bogs, this European spider catches and feasts on fish. A white stripe runs along the side of its abdomen.

Its body can change color to match the flower it sits on.

⑥ Camouflaged perfectly on flowers, this brightly colored spider ambushes passing prey. It scuttles sideways like the sea creature after which it is named.

⑦ Weighing up to 6 oz (170 g) and with a leg span of 12 in (30 cm), this is the largest spider in the world. It uses its fangs to hunt frogs and mice in the Amazon rainforest.

Hairs on its legs detect the vibrations of moving prey.

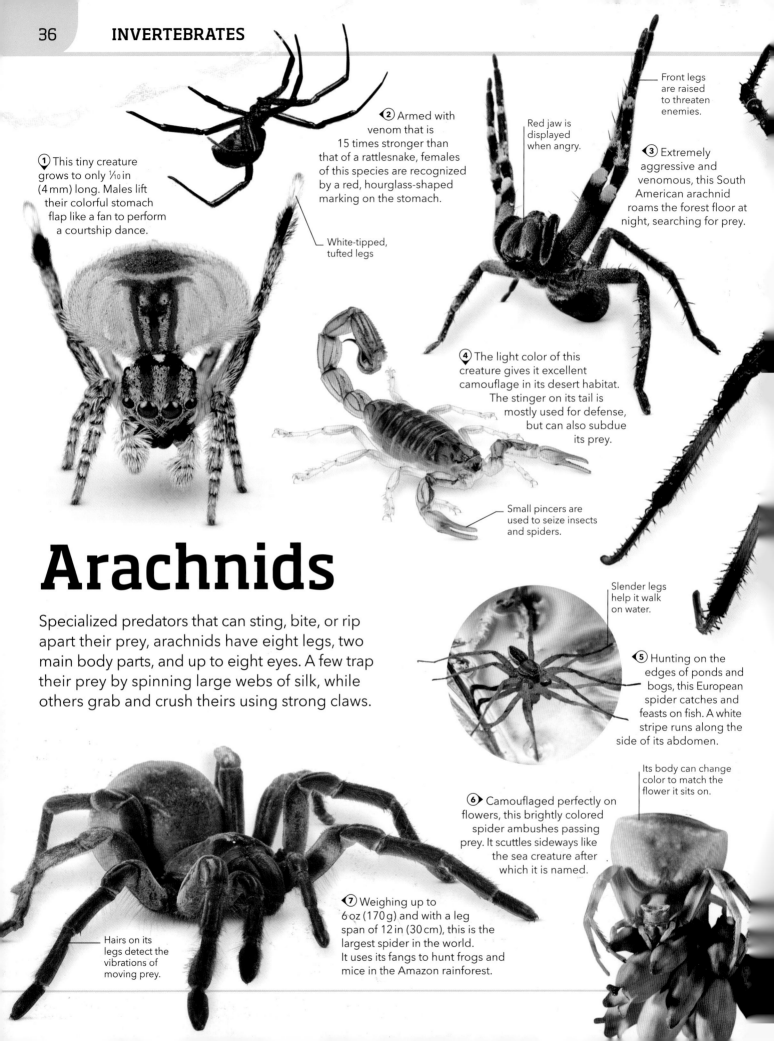

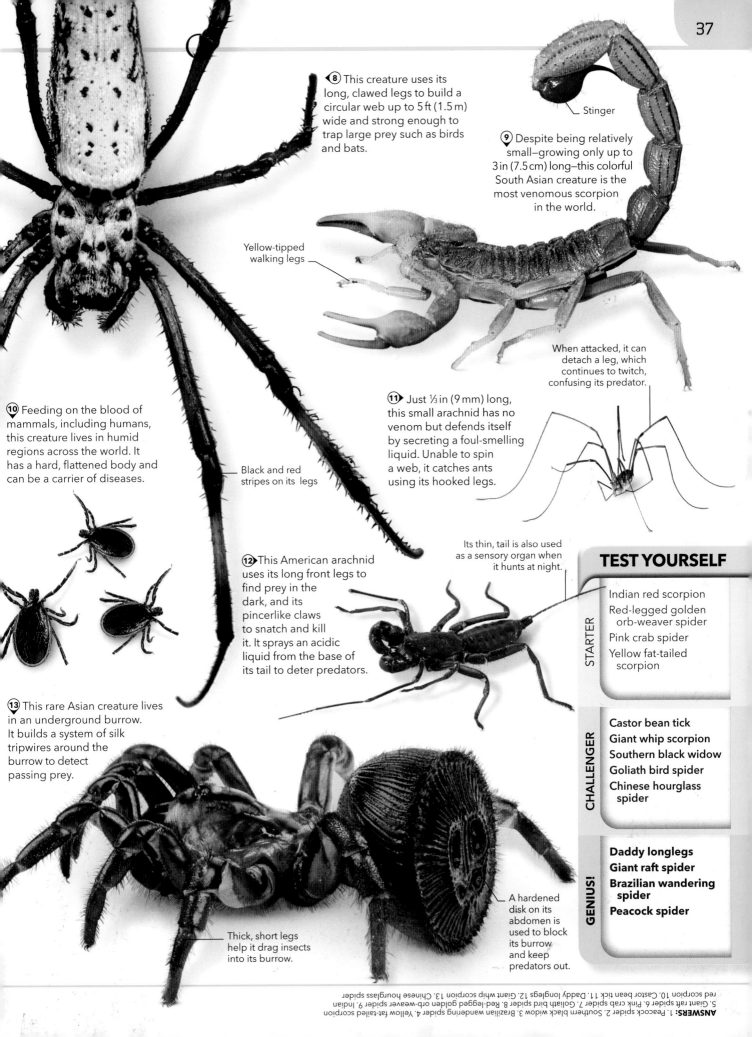

Stinger

8 This creature uses its long, clawed legs to build a circular web up to 5 ft (1.5 m) wide and strong enough to trap large prey such as birds and bats.

9 Despite being relatively small—growing only up to 3 in (7.5 cm) long—this colorful South Asian creature is the most venomous scorpion in the world.

Yellow-tipped walking legs

When attacked, it can detach a leg, which continues to twitch, confusing its predator.

10 Feeding on the blood of mammals, including humans, this creature lives in humid regions across the world. It has a hard, flattened body and can be a carrier of diseases.

11 Just ⅓ in (9 mm) long, this small arachnid has no venom but defends itself by secreting a foul-smelling liquid. Unable to spin a web, it catches ants using its hooked legs.

Black and red stripes on its legs

12 This American arachnid uses its long front legs to find prey in the dark, and its pincerlike claws to snatch and kill it. It sprays an acidic liquid from the base of its tail to deter predators.

Its thin, tail is also used as a sensory organ when it hunts at night.

13 This rare Asian creature lives in an underground burrow. It builds a system of silk tripwires around the burrow to detect passing prey.

Thick, short legs help it drag insects into its burrow.

A hardened disk on its abdomen is used to block its burrow and keep predators out.

TEST YOURSELF

STARTER
- Indian red scorpion
- Red-legged golden orb-weaver spider
- Pink crab spider
- Yellow fat-tailed scorpion

CHALLENGER
- **Castor bean tick**
- **Giant whip scorpion**
- **Southern black widow**
- **Goliath bird spider**
- **Chinese hourglass spider**

GENIUS!
- **Daddy longlegs**
- **Giant raft spider**
- **Brazilian wandering spider**
- **Peacock spider**

An insect's body is divided into three sections: head, abdomen, and thorax—the section between the head and the abdomen. Most insects have six legs and four wings. Most of them can fly. There are around 30 main insect groups—here are six of them.

The delicate wings of beetles are protected by hard cases called elytra.

Beetles
With more than 300,000 species known so far—about a quarter of all animal species—this is the largest group of insects in the world.

Bugs
The insects in this group, including aphids, stink bugs, and leafhoppers, use their tubelike mouths to suck up food.

Moths and butterflies
Colorful wings make these the most recognizable garden insects. They begin their lives as caterpillars.

Insects

Small in size and protected by hard external shells called exoskeletons, insects can survive in different habitats, from scorching deserts to the freezing Antarctic. For every one person on Earth, there are as many as 1.4 billion insects!

BEETLE BOMB

When threatened, a bombardier beetle squirts boiling, toxic liquid at its attacker from the rear end of its abdomen.

How to pollinate a flower

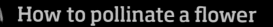

01. When you go looking for sweet nectar to make honey, you help pollinate flowers. So look for a colorful flower with lots of nectar and pollen.

02. As you drink the nectar, some of the pollen will attach itself to your body and legs. You can now fly away to another flower. You will need to visit thousands of flowers each day to gather enough nectar.

Pollen collected in baskets on legs

03. When you land on the other flower, rub the pollen from your legs onto it. Seeds can now develop, because when pollen from one flower is passed to another, it fertilizes the flower and makes it produce seeds.

Crickets and grasshoppers
These insects produce unique chirping sounds by rubbing their body parts together.

Wasps, ants, and bees
The members of this group have narrow "waists" and many live in colonies.

Flies
Found almost everywhere on Earth, these insects are an important source of food for birds, fish, and mammals.

I don't believe it !
Dragonflies have compound eyes made up of up to 30,000 tiny detectors that can sense small changes in brightness and color in their environment.

🪲 The desert locust is one of the most destructive insects on the planet. In only a few hours, a swarm of 40–80 million insects, packed in $\frac{1}{3}$ sq mile (1 sq km), can eat enough grain to feed 35,000 people for a day.

🪲 The shrill thorn tree cicada is the loudest insect in the world. It can produce a sound that measures 106 decibels— that is as loud as a chainsaw!

🪲 Fleas are expert leapers, and can jump up to 150 times their own height in a single bound!

Wonderful wings

Hidden predator: The spiny flower mantis uses its colorful wings to mimic a flower and lure in its prey.

Expert flier: The wings of dragonflies, like this red marsh glider, help them fly up, down, and from side to side.

Iridescent wings: The Madagascan sunset moth's wings are covered in tiny scales, which shimmer with rainbow colors.

Bright defenses: The checkered beetle has brightly patterned wing cases that may warn predators to stay away.

Colossal colonies

Termites live together in large groups, or colonies, of up to one million individuals. They are master builders and can construct mud mounds over 33 ft (10 m) tall–more than five times the height of an adult human.

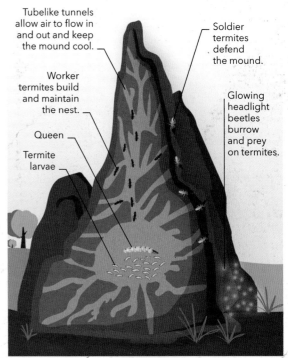

Tubelike tunnels allow air to flow in and out and keep the mound cool.

Worker termites build and maintain the nest.

Queen

Termite larvae

Soldier termites defend the mound.

Glowing headlight beetles burrow and prey on termites.

Heavy lifting

Weighing a whopping $1\frac{3}{4}$ oz (50 g)–about as much as a golf ball–the goliath beetle is one of the largest insects in the world. It can lift objects 850 times its own weight!

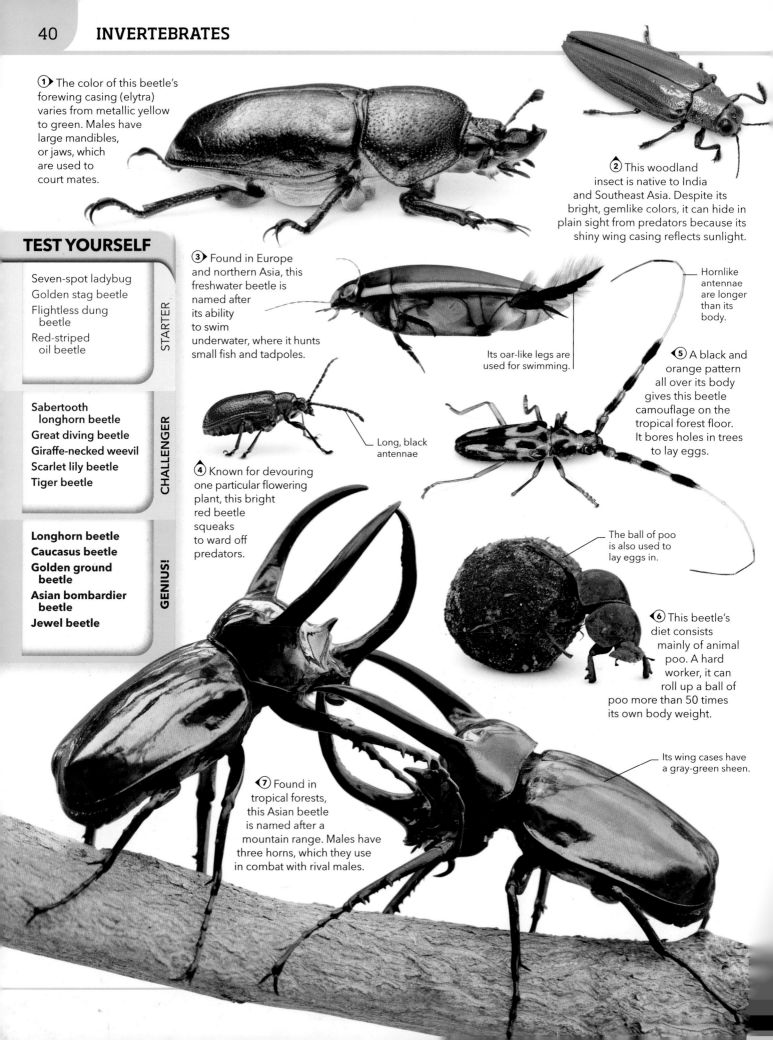

1 The color of this beetle's forewing casing (elytra) varies from metallic yellow to green. Males have large mandibles, or jaws, which are used to court mates.

2 This woodland insect is native to India and Southeast Asia. Despite its bright, gemlike colors, it can hide in plain sight from predators because its shiny wing casing reflects sunlight.

TEST YOURSELF

STARTER
- Seven-spot ladybug
- Golden stag beetle
- Flightless dung beetle
- Red-striped oil beetle

CHALLENGER
- Sabertooth longhorn beetle
- Great diving beetle
- Giraffe-necked weevil
- Scarlet lily beetle
- Tiger beetle

GENIUS!
- Longhorn beetle
- Caucasus beetle
- Golden ground beetle
- Asian bombardier beetle
- Jewel beetle

3 Found in Europe and northern Asia, this freshwater beetle is named after its ability to swim underwater, where it hunts small fish and tadpoles.

Its oar-like legs are used for swimming.

Hornlike antennae are longer than its body.

5 A black and orange pattern all over its body gives this beetle camouflage on the tropical forest floor. It bores holes in trees to lay eggs.

Long, black antennae

4 Known for devouring one particular flowering plant, this bright red beetle squeaks to ward off predators.

The ball of poo is also used to lay eggs in.

6 This beetle's diet consists mainly of animal poo. A hard worker, it can roll up a ball of poo more than 50 times its own body weight.

Its wing cases have a gray-green sheen.

7 Found in tropical forests, this Asian beetle is named after a mountain range. Males have three horns, which they use in combat with rival males.

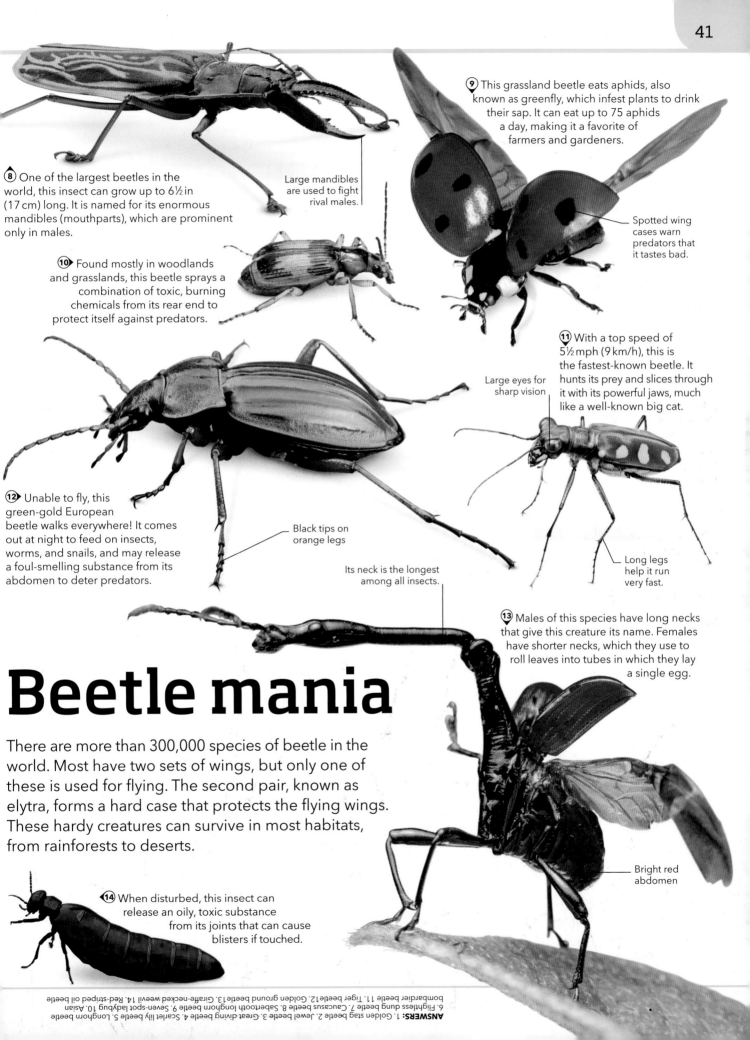

⑨ This grassland beetle eats aphids, also known as greenfly, which infest plants to drink their sap. It can eat up to 75 aphids a day, making it a favorite of farmers and gardeners.

⑧ One of the largest beetles in the world, this insect can grow up to 6½ in (17 cm) long. It is named for its enormous mandibles (mouthparts), which are prominent only in males.

Large mandibles are used to fight rival males.

Spotted wing cases warn predators that it tastes bad.

⑩ Found mostly in woodlands and grasslands, this beetle sprays a combination of toxic, burning chemicals from its rear end to protect itself against predators.

⑪ With a top speed of 5½ mph (9 km/h), this is the fastest-known beetle. It hunts its prey and slices through it with its powerful jaws, much like a well-known big cat.

Large eyes for sharp vision

⑫ Unable to fly, this green-gold European beetle walks everywhere! It comes out at night to feed on insects, worms, and snails, and may release a foul-smelling substance from its abdomen to deter predators.

Black tips on orange legs

Long legs help it run very fast.

Its neck is the longest among all insects.

⑬ Males of this species have long necks that give this creature its name. Females have shorter necks, which they use to roll leaves into tubes in which they lay a single egg.

Beetle mania

There are more than 300,000 species of beetle in the world. Most have two sets of wings, but only one of these is used for flying. The second pair, known as elytra, forms a hard case that protects the flying wings. These hardy creatures can survive in most habitats, from rainforests to deserts.

Bright red abdomen

⑭ When disturbed, this insect can release an oily, toxic substance from its joints that can cause blisters if touched.

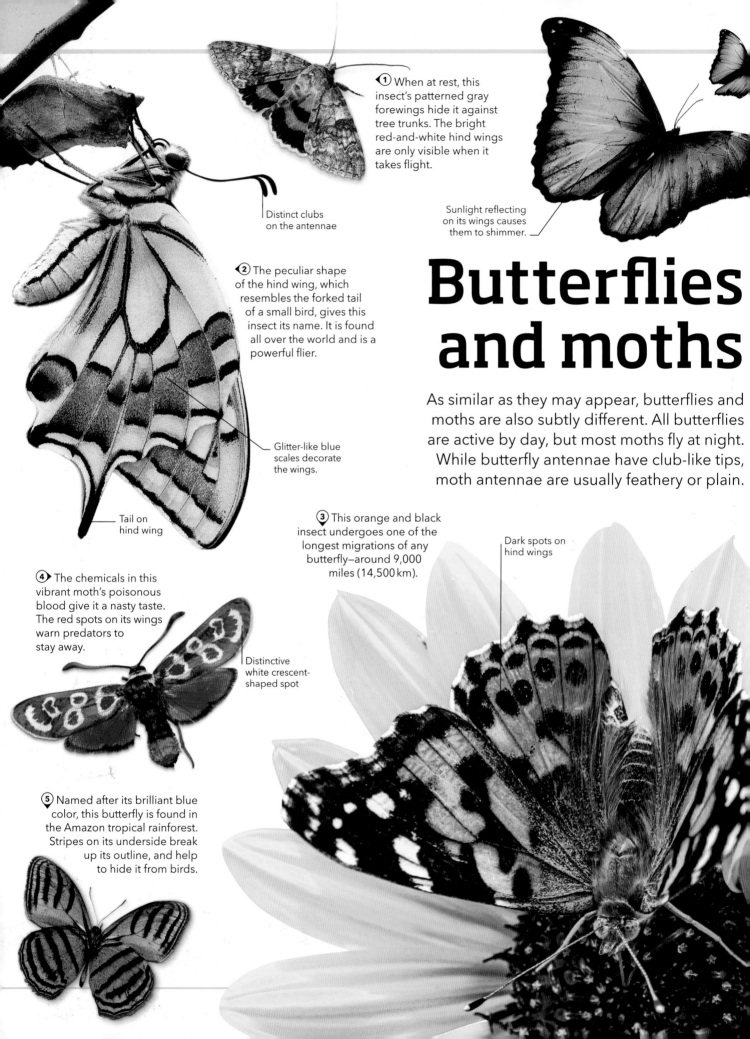

1 When at rest, this insect's patterned gray forewings hide it against tree trunks. The bright red-and-white hind wings are only visible when it takes flight.

Distinct clubs on the antennae

Sunlight reflecting on its wings causes them to shimmer.

2 The peculiar shape of the hind wing, which resembles the forked tail of a small bird, gives this insect its name. It is found all over the world and is a powerful flier.

Butterflies and moths

As similar as they may appear, butterflies and moths are also subtly different. All butterflies are active by day, but most moths fly at night. While butterfly antennae have club-like tips, moth antennae are usually feathery or plain.

Glitter-like blue scales decorate the wings.

Tail on hind wing

3 This orange and black insect undergoes one of the longest migrations of any butterfly—around 9,000 miles (14,500 km).

Dark spots on hind wings

4 The chemicals in this vibrant moth's poisonous blood give it a nasty taste. The red spots on its wings warn predators to stay away.

Distinctive white crescent-shaped spot

5 Named after its brilliant blue color, this butterfly is found in the Amazon tropical rainforest. Stripes on its underside break up its outline, and help to hide it from birds.

7 Named for the fine thread made by its caterpillars, this stout, hairy insect is native to China but is now found across the world.

Its wings are too small for flight.

Pink hind wing

Black and white checks on body

6 Found in South America, with a wingspan of up to 8 in (20 cm), this is one of the largest butterflies in the world. When it perches in the shade, it closes its wings to hide the bright blue color from predators.

8 Hovering from flower to flower to feed on nectar with its long proboscis (tubelike mouthpart), this moth looks almost like a tiny bird.

Peacock-like eyespots on every wing

Large, feathery antennae help males detect scents given off by females.

9 Males of this royal species have an amazing sense of smell and can pick up a female's scent from 5 miles (8 km) away.

11 Named after the number-like shapes on its wings, this creature is considered by some to symbolize good fortune in its native Central and South America.

10 This insect is found on the Indian subcontinent. The tails on its wings are crucial to its survival. Birds see these first and peck them, leaving the head and body alone.

12 This butterfly is one of the largest in Australia and is named after the city near which it is found. It has a large wingspan of up to 6 in (15 cm) from tip to tip.

Three tails on each hind wing

13 Native to the Mediterranean region, this insect likes to rest during the day and emerge at night to feed on nectar from flowers.

Males are smaller than females but more colorful.

Clear wings make it difficult to spot in flight.

The leafy green color helps it hide from birds and lizards.

14 Unlike other butterflies, whose wings are covered with overlapping scales, this species has scales only on the edges of its wings, making them transparent. As a result, it is almost invisible to predators.

Complete metamorphosis

After a caterpillar hatches from its egg, it starts to eat and grows bigger, molting its skin several times. When it is big enough, an amazing transformation begins.

It takes two hours for a butterfly to fly off after emerging from its chrysalis.

Hanging from a twig, the caterpillar produces a hard layer of skin, or chrysalis, around itself. Within this layer, it transforms into a butterfly.

As the butterfly emerges from the chrysalis, it hangs upside down to dry and expand its wrinkled wings.

Insect life cycles

Most insects lay eggs, which then develop in two different ways. One is a complete change, or metamorphosis, as seen when a caterpillar transforms into a butterfly. The other is an incomplete metamorphosis as in the case of a dragonfly, where the baby looks like a smaller adult and sheds its skin as it grows.

I don't believe it

The larva of the six-spot burnet moth can protect itself by secreting a liquid that can glue together the jaws and legs of predators.

How to become an adult dragonfly

03. Your newly formed skin is soft, which makes it easy for you to squeeze out. Your new skin will harden over time.

02. Start to wriggle as your old skin splits open, to release yourself from the hard outer shell.

01. Once you have hatched into a nymph, climb out of the pond and cling to a reed. Prepare to transform.

All grown up!

Unlike humans, baby insects often look nothing like the adults they grow into. Take a look at the insects below and their amazing transformation from larvae to adults.

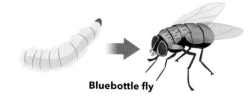

Bluebottle fly

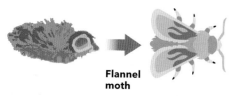

Flannel moth

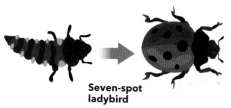

Seven-spot ladybird

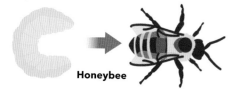

Honeybee

In numbers

50
The number of years a queen termite can live.

500
The number of eggs a housefly can lay in a four-day period.

5/8 mile
(1 km) The length of silk thread used to make the cocoon of a silkworm moth.

A QUEEN'S LIFE
Queen termites have been known to lay one egg a second—that adds up to 30 million eggs a year!

Monarch migration

Every fall, monarch butterflies embark on a 3,000-mile (4,800-km) journey from the northern US and Canada to Mexico. These butterflies will never return north.

In spring, the next generation of these butterflies hatch and start making the journey back north.

Monarch butterflies use air currents to help them make the long journeys.

These butterflies have never made this journey before. They rely on instinct to find their way.

Dragonflies mate and catch prey in mid-air!

04. Your shriveled wings slowly start to expand as you get ready for your first flight.

05. You are now an adult! Your transformation from a nymph to a dragonfly has taken around 75 minutes.

Long antennae used to find food.

2▶ Marching through forests in columns with military precision, this destructive insect will eat anything in its path. Its swarms can kill up to 100,000 animals in a day, including other insects, chickens, snakes, and even birds.

① Just 1 in (2.5 cm) long, this insect may be small, but it is fearsome. It has one of the most painful stings in the world—often described as like being shot!

③ The queens of this species from Asia can reach up to 2 in (5 cm) in length, making it one of the largest wasps in the world. It likes to hunt and kill honeybees.

Long, segmented antennae are used to communicate with each other.

Winged wonders

A nest, called a bivouac, is made of thousands of individuals.

Bees, wasps, and ants all belong to a group of insects called hymenoptera, which means "membrane wings." This group includes important pollinators that are essential to life on Earth. Buzzing across the garden, darting from flower to flower, bees and wasps also help humans grow fruits and vegetables.

◀④ This wasp defends its nest by beating its wings furiously. It is aggressive in its display and will sting only as a last resort because if it uses its stinger, it will die.

A tubelike organ is used for drilling into wood.

Sensitive antennae detect hidden prey.

Blue-black metallic sheen on the body

⑤ Females of this species lay a single egg inside other insects. The larva then feeds on and kills the host insect, and emerges fully grown.

Its color serves as a warning to predators.

Its long legs allow it to escape quickly when disturbed.

6 This critter is named for its bright color and fluffy fur. The females (pictured) are wingless and often mistaken for ants.

7 This creature is found all over the world and can often be seen disturbing picnics. Despite its reputation for aggressive behavior, this insect is an effective controller of pests, eating flies and other insects.

8 This insect has a very big, armored head, which it can use like a door to block the entrance to its nest. It can also pull its antennae and legs under its head for protection.

Worker bees have white tails at the tip.

9 The body of this insect appears to be a blue-green metallic color, while its tail gleams like a precious gemstone. It lays its eggs in the nests of other insects.

11 When in danger, this insect strikes a defensive pose—opening its jaws and curling its stomach downward. This is followed by spraying acid on its enemy.

10 Buzzing from flower to flower, this insect gathers nectar, in turn pollinating plants. It lives in colonies with up to 80,000 members, all of which work for a queen.

12 Sometimes called a "nectar robber," this bee bites a hole in flowers to suck out their juice. Its queen has a distinctively colored tail.

Eyes are made up of lots of tiny lenses.

13 Often seen in backyards, this ant lives in colonies that produce winged males and females in the summer mating season.

TEST YOURSELF

STARTER	CHALLENGER	GENIUS!
Western honeybee	**Asian giant hornet**	**Northern warrior wasp**
Common black ant	**Buff-tailed bumblebee**	**Ichneumon wasp**
Common wasp	**Ruby-tailed wasp**	**Bullet ant**
Red velvet wasp	**Turtle ant**	**Red wood ant**
Army ant		

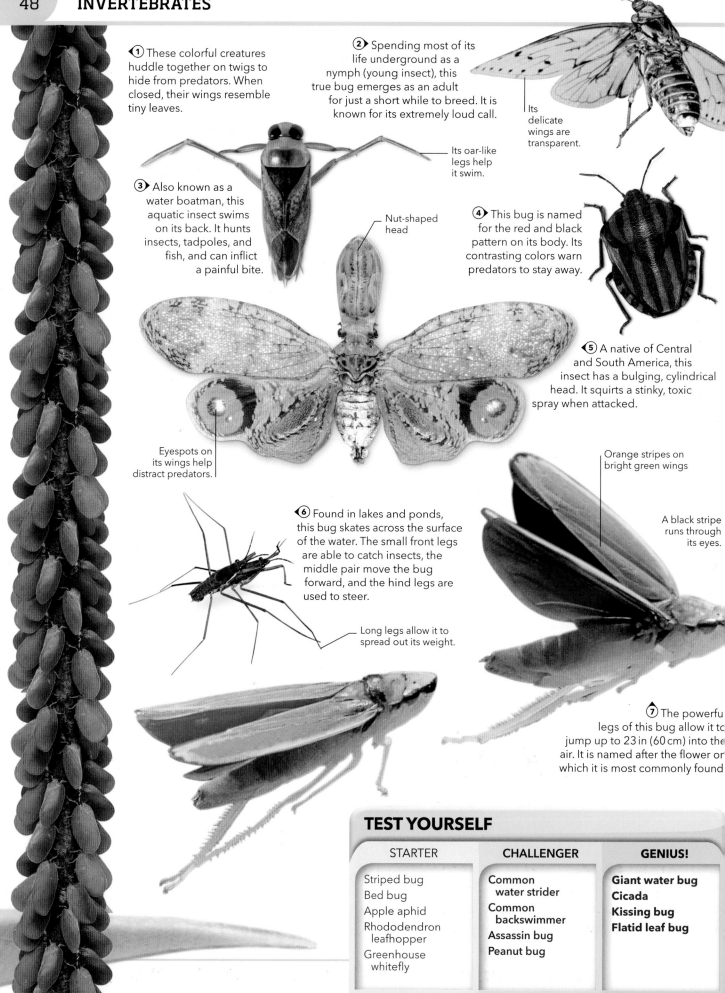

1 These colorful creatures huddle together on twigs to hide from predators. When closed, their wings resemble tiny leaves.

2 Spending most of its life underground as a nymph (young insect), this true bug emerges as an adult for just a short while to breed. It is known for its extremely loud call.

Its delicate wings are transparent.

3 Also known as a water boatman, this aquatic insect swims on its back. It hunts insects, tadpoles, and fish, and can inflict a painful bite.

Its oar-like legs help it swim.

Nut-shaped head

4 This bug is named for the red and black pattern on its body. Its contrasting colors warn predators to stay away.

5 A native of Central and South America, this insect has a bulging, cylindrical head. It squirts a stinky, toxic spray when attacked.

Eyespots on its wings help distract predators.

6 Found in lakes and ponds, this bug skates across the surface of the water. The small front legs are able to catch insects, the middle pair move the bug forward, and the hind legs are used to steer.

Long legs allow it to spread out its weight.

Orange stripes on bright green wings

A black stripe runs through its eyes.

7 The powerful legs of this bug allow it to jump up to 23 in (60 cm) into the air. It is named after the flower on which it is most commonly found.

TEST YOURSELF

STARTER	CHALLENGER	GENIUS!
Striped bug	**Common water strider**	**Giant water bug**
Bed bug		**Cicada**
Apple aphid	**Common backswimmer**	**Kissing bug**
Rhododendron leafhopper	**Assassin bug**	**Flatid leaf bug**
Greenhouse whitefly	**Peanut bug**	

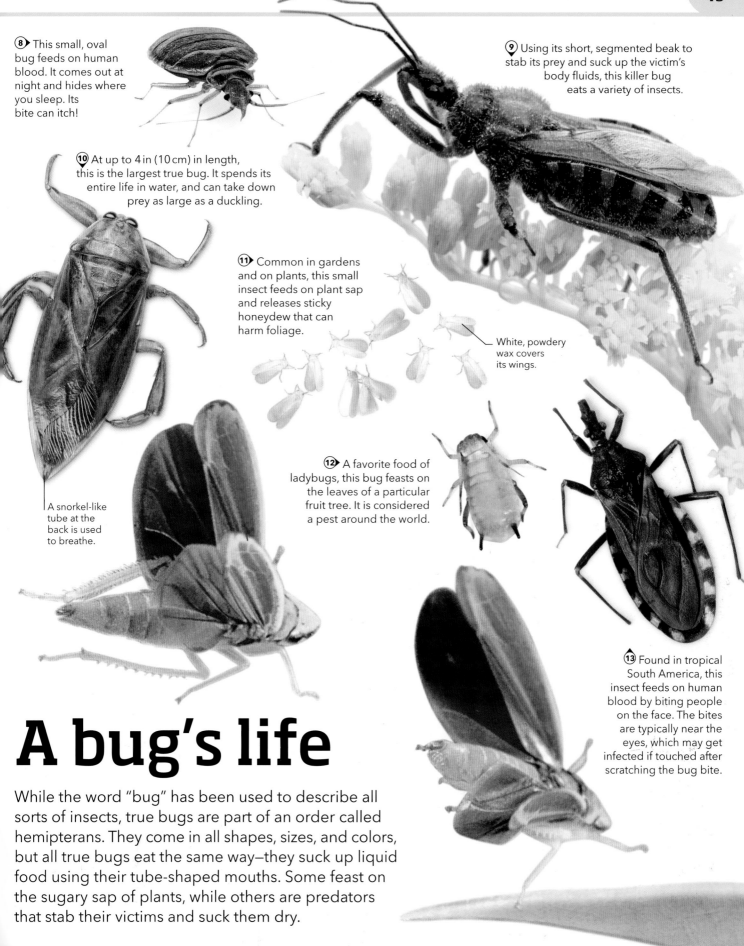

8 This small, oval bug feeds on human blood. It comes out at night and hides where you sleep. Its bite can itch!

9 Using its short, segmented beak to stab its prey and suck up the victim's body fluids, this killer bug eats a variety of insects.

10 At up to 4 in (10 cm) in length, this is the largest true bug. It spends its entire life in water, and can take down prey as large as a duckling.

11 Common in gardens and on plants, this small insect feeds on plant sap and releases sticky honeydew that can harm foliage.

White, powdery wax covers its wings.

12 A favorite food of ladybugs, this bug feasts on the leaves of a particular fruit tree. It is considered a pest around the world.

A snorkel-like tube at the back is used to breathe.

13 Found in tropical South America, this insect feeds on human blood by biting people on the face. The bites are typically near the eyes, which may get infected if touched after scratching the bug bite.

A bug's life

While the word "bug" has been used to describe all sorts of insects, true bugs are part of an order called hemipterans. They come in all shapes, sizes, and colors, but all true bugs eat the same way—they suck up liquid food using their tube-shaped mouths. Some feast on the sugary sap of plants, while others are predators that stab their victims and suck them dry.

ANSWERS: 1. Flatid leaf bug 2. Cicada 3. Common backswimmer 4. Striped bug 5. Peanut bug 6. Common water strider 7. Rhododendron leafhopper 8. Bed bug 9. Assassin bug 10. Giant water bug 11. Greenhouse whitefly 12. Apple aphid 13. Kissing bug

1 With a brown-and-green body that gives excellent camouflage on the trunk of a tree, this tropical insect blends into the bark to avoid being eaten by predators, such as bats and birds.

Strong hind legs help it climb.

2 This African creature looks like a withered leaf. This makes it almost impossible to spot on the forest floor, where it plays dead to hide from predators passing by.

Hide and seek

Some insects have the incredible ability to mimic their surroundings so well that they can hide in plain sight from their predators as well as prey. As always, the challenge is to identify the insects, but you have got to find them first!

Long hind legs for jumping across long distances.

3 Most at home on trees covered by small green plants in South American rainforests, this insect uses its antennae to look for leaves and grass to eat.

4 With bodies shaped like the spines of plants, these American insects huddle together on branches and suck up the sap—safely hidden from birds looking for a meal.

Its brown body makes it resemble wood.

5 A thin, twiglike body gives this insect perfect camouflage on the slender tree on which it perches. Females of this African species can grow up to 13 in (33 cm) long.

Veins on its wings resemble those of leaves.

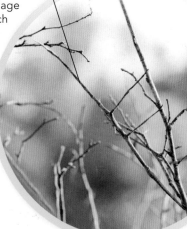

6 The wings of this South Asian creature only reveal its beautiful, bright colors when they are open. When the wings are closed, they enable it to hide on branches by mimicking dry foliage on the brink of dropping to the ground.

ANSWERS: 1. Katydid 2. Ghost mantis 3. Moss mimic bush cricket 4. Thorn bug 5. Madagascan stick insect 6. Indian leaf butterfly 7. Green shield bug 8. Orchid mantis 9. Rock locust 10. Caribbean wafer cockroach 11. Buff-tip moth 12. Leaf insect 13. Baron caterpillar

7 This European insect easily blends among leaves because of its color. When disturbed, it produces a stinky liquid as a form of defense.

Broad, knobbly body

8 Flat, petallike appendages make this insect look like a flower while it waits for its prey. This deadly disguise allows it to hide from insects that come to the flower to feed, and then snatch them out of the air once they are close enough.

Thin, hairy spines disguise its outline.

9 Found in the rugged deserts of southern Africa, this insect conceals itself from hungry predators by blending into the landscape.

10 The flat, ridged, brown body of this hardy tropical creature helps it hide from predators by merging into the dried leaves it eats on the forest floor.

Light-colored patch at the tip of its wings

11 When at rest, the wings of this flying insect are held against its body and give it a striking resemblance to a broken birch twig.

Furry head

12 Closely related to stick insects, this tropical creature has a deep green coloring, which gives it very good camouflage on green plants.

13 Found on the leaves of mango trees, this insect has a pale stripe along the center of its body that blends into the leaf's central vein, making it almost entirely invisible to birds.

TEST YOURSELF

STARTER	CHALLENGER	GENIUS!
Madagascan stick insect	Moss mimic bush cricket	Baron caterpillar
Leaf insect	Thorn bug	Buff-tip moth
Orchid mantis	Green shield bug	Katydid
Indian leaf butterfly	Rock locust	Ghost mantis
	Caribbean wafer cockroach	

3

FISH

Swirling school
Near the Revillagigedo Archipelago in the Pacific Ocean, smaller fish, such as rainbow chub, bunch together in a large formation known as a bait ball. This form of defense makes it hard for their attackers, including sharks and tuna, to pick off individual fish.

Types of fish

Jawless fish
With muscular mouths and no jaw bones, these were the very first fish. They consist of two families—lampreys (shown) and hagfish—which together make up around 120 species.

Bony fish
The skeletons of these fish are made of hard bone. There are more than 28,000 species of bony fish, with a wide range of shapes and sizes.

Cartilaginous fish
These fish have skeletons made of tough, flexible tissue known as cartilage. Sharks, rays, and chimeras are cartilaginous fish.

What is a fish?

A fish is a cold-blooded animal that lives under water and uses organs called gills to breathe. Most fish have scaly skin and several sets of fins.

Dorsal fins keep the fish stable and help it swim straight.

Bony skeleton

The tail fin sweeps from side to side, pushing the fish forward.

Anal fins help balance the fish while swimming.

Gills are rows of tiny, blood-filled tubes which allow the fish to absorb oxygen from the water that enters its mouth.

Gills take in oxygen

Water flows in

Fish

Around 500 million years ago, the first animals with internal skeletons appeared–fish. Today, they make up almost half of all vertebrates. Fish come in many shapes and sizes, from tiny seahorses to the giant whale shark, but typically have a streamlined body and strong muscles for moving through the water.

I don't believe it!

When a hagfish is threatened, it squirts slime from pores along the sides of its body, making it slippery and difficult to catch.

In numbers

100 million
The number of herring that can swim together in a group, called a mega shoal.

9 million
The number of eggs a female cod can produce in one year.

300
The number of teeth a great white shark may have at one time, arranged in seven rows inside its mouth.

How to court a mate like a puffer fish

01. Use your belly to carefully arrange sand on the seabed to form a perfect circle up to 7 ft (2 m) in diameter.

02. Swim repeatedly in straight lines from the outside of the circle to its center, waving your fins to create small peaks.

Page 55

Swimming styles

All fish bend, move, and stretch the muscles attached to their backbones to move through water. However, the swimming style varies from species to species.

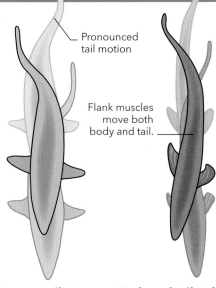

Pronounced tail motion

Flank muscles move both body and tail.

Its side-to-side, rippling movement pushes it forward.

Side to side: Long fish, including eels, move like a snake, bending their bodies as they swim.

Strong tail: Some fish, such as tuna, move their tail fins rapidly to swim at high speeds.

Body and tail: A fish like a salmon moves its body and tail in unison, allowing for quick turns.

The female lays its eggs in the sand for days, which the male fertilizes and guards for days.

04. When a potential mate approaches, stir the nest's sand to show her its quality. Then rush toward her and retreat into the nest. If she likes what she sees, she will join you in the circle and mate with you.

03. Using your anal fin, draw thin lines across the center of the circle, and hope it catches a female's eye! If your structure is swept away by ocean currents, build it again.

Birth stories

Egg guardian: The common ghost goby lays its eggs on soft corals or sponges. It stays with the eggs, keeping an eye out for predators until they hatch.

Mouth brooder: The male yellow-headed jawfish keeps fertilized eggs safe inside his mouth. He cannot eat until they have hatched!

Armored eggs: The lesser-spotted dogfish lays eggs with tough, leathery cases. Long tendrils anchor the cases to plants.

Live-bearer: The lemon shark gives birth to live young. Babies swim away from their mothers quickly to avoid being eaten.

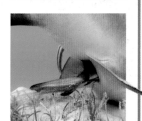

Pouch protector: The male seahorse keeps its eggs in a pouch on its stomach. Once the eggs hatch, babies are released into the water.

Toxic tactics

⚠ The poison from one puffer fish can kill 30 humans. At present, it does not have an antidote.

⚠ Lionfish have venom in their spines, which can cause an allergic reaction in humans.

⚠ When threatened, a stonefish (pictured) can use its dorsal spines to inject predators with a deadly venom.

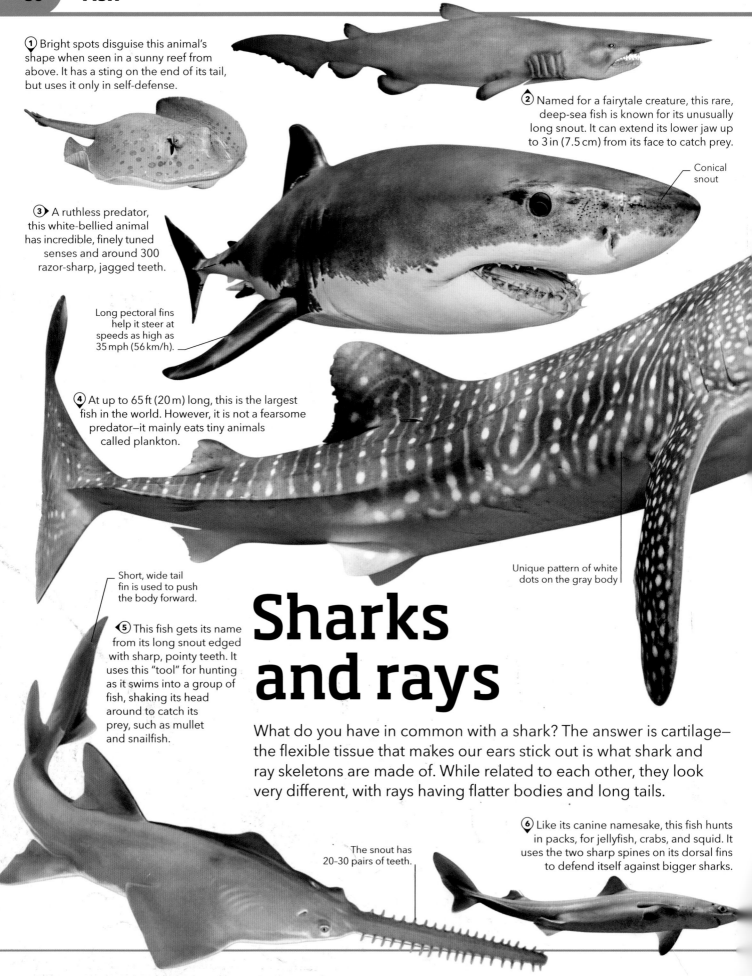

① Bright spots disguise this animal's shape when seen in a sunny reef from above. It has a sting on the end of its tail, but uses it only in self-defense.

② Named for a fairytale creature, this rare, deep-sea fish is known for its unusually long snout. It can extend its lower jaw up to 3 in (7.5 cm) from its face to catch prey.

Conical snout

③ A ruthless predator, this white-bellied animal has incredible, finely tuned senses and around 300 razor-sharp, jagged teeth.

Long pectoral fins help it steer at speeds as high as 35 mph (56 km/h).

④ At up to 65 ft (20 m) long, this is the largest fish in the world. However, it is not a fearsome predator—it mainly eats tiny animals called plankton.

Unique pattern of white dots on the gray body

Short, wide tail fin is used to push the body forward.

⑤ This fish gets its name from its long snout edged with sharp, pointy teeth. It uses this "tool" for hunting as it swims into a group of fish, shaking its head around to catch its prey, such as mullet and snailfish.

Sharks and rays

What do you have in common with a shark? The answer is cartilage—the flexible tissue that makes our ears stick out is what shark and ray skeletons are made of. While related to each other, they look very different, with rays having flatter bodies and long tails.

The snout has 20–30 pairs of teeth.

⑥ Like its canine namesake, this fish hunts in packs, for jellyfish, crabs, and squid. It uses the two sharp spines on its dorsal fins to defend itself against bigger sharks.

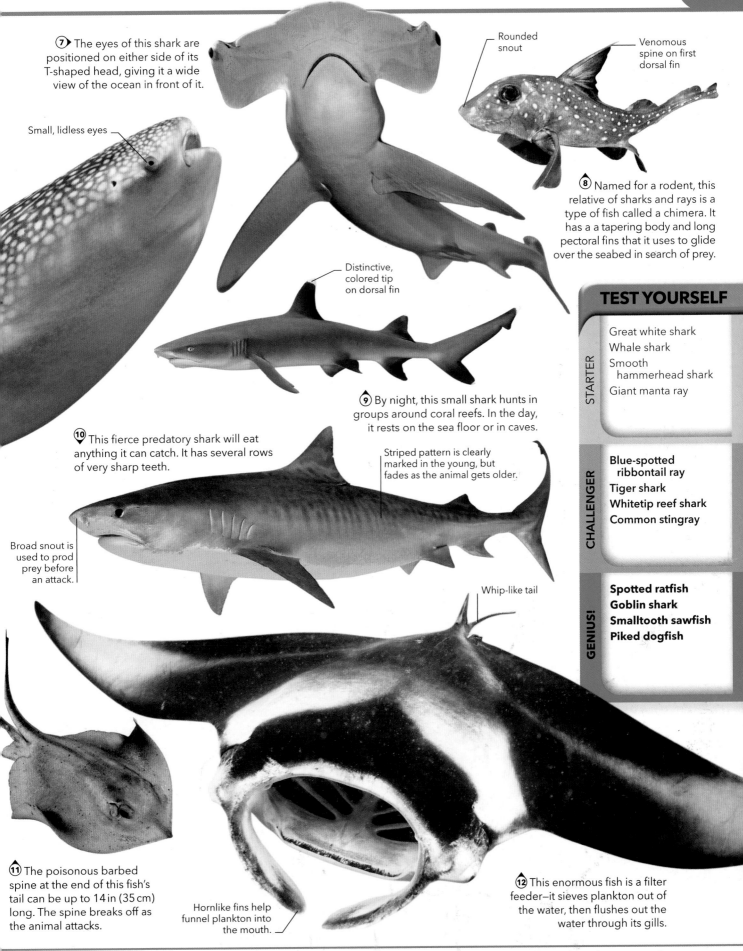

7 The eyes of this shark are positioned on either side of its T-shaped head, giving it a wide view of the ocean in front of it.

Small, lidless eyes

Rounded snout

Venomous spine on first dorsal fin

8 Named for a rodent, this relative of sharks and rays is a type of fish called a chimera. It has a tapering body and long pectoral fins that it uses to glide over the seabed in search of prey.

Distinctive, colored tip on dorsal fin

9 By night, this small shark hunts in groups around coral reefs. In the day, it rests on the sea floor or in caves.

10 This fierce predatory shark will eat anything it can catch. It has several rows of very sharp teeth.

Striped pattern is clearly marked in the young, but fades as the animal gets older.

Broad snout is used to prod prey before an attack.

Whip-like tail

11 The poisonous barbed spine at the end of this fish's tail can be up to 14 in (35 cm) long. The spine breaks off as the animal attacks.

Hornlike fins help funnel plankton into the mouth.

12 This enormous fish is a filter feeder—it sieves plankton out of the water, then flushes out the water through its gills.

TEST YOURSELF

STARTER
- Great white shark
- Whale shark
- Smooth hammerhead shark
- Giant manta ray

CHALLENGER
- Blue-spotted ribbontail ray
- Tiger shark
- Whitetip reef shark
- Common stingray

GENIUS!
- Spotted ratfish
- Goblin shark
- Smalltooth sawfish
- Piked dogfish

ANSWERS: 1. Blue-spotted ribbontail ray 2. Goblin shark 3. Great white shark 4. Whale shark 5. Smalltooth sawfish 6. Piked dogfish 7. Smooth hammerhead shark 8. Spotted ratfish 9. Whitetip reef shark 10. Tiger shark 11. Common stingray 12. Giant manta ray

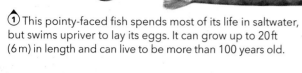

1 This pointy-faced fish spends most of its life in saltwater, but swims upriver to lay its eggs. It can grow up to 20 ft (6 m) in length and can live to be more than 100 years old.

Sensitive, whisker-like barbels help detect prey.

2 Buried in the sand, this flatfish remains motionless during the day, making it hard to spot. At night, it leaves its hiding place to feed on shrimp. It is commonly found in the Atlantic Ocean around France, Belgium, the UK, and Ireland.

Bright orange spots

Bony fish

From the enormous sunfish to tiny seahorses, bony fish come in all shapes and sizes. They have a hard skeleton and a swim bladder (sac filled with gas) that helps them stay afloat. There are at least 32,000 species of bony fish. They live in all kinds of waters, from shallow ponds and rivers to vast oceans.

Sail-like dorsal fin can be lowered when swimming at high speeds.

3 Named after a well-known spotted predator, this creature hides in coral reefs and waits for prey to swim past. It then quickly darts out, seizing its meal with sharp teeth.

Long, pointed bill

A single fin runs from its head, around the tail, and up to its underbelly.

Instead of a tail, this fish has a frilly rudder-like flap.

Thick stripes on body

4 This fish is tiny—around ¾ in (2 cm) long. Its bright colors help it blend into its reef habitat as it keeps its tail tightly coiled around coral to keep from being swept away.

6 The heaviest bony fish in the world, this animal weighs about 2 tons—as much as a rhinoceros! It enjoys sunning itself near the water's surface.

7 This long and slender fish hunts along the bottom of South American rivers, looking for smaller fish to eat. Its long whiskers help it detect prey in the dark.

Crest of long, bright red rays on head

5 Longest of all known bony fish, this creature's ribbonlike body can reach more than 30 ft (9 m) in length. It has inspired legends of giant sea serpents.

8 These large, colorful fish use their birdlike beaks to graze on the algae that live on coral reefs. They often swim together, in big groups of around 40 fish.

Females use a luminous "lure" on their heads to tempt prey close enough to catch.

9 Round and with jellylike flesh, this fish lives in the deep, dark regions of the ocean. Females are much larger than males.

Strong, flexible scales protect against piranha attacks.

Body can weigh up to 440 lb (200 kg).

10 Taking in oxygen from the air instead of the water means this South American freshwater fish must visit the water's surface to breathe. As it does this it makes a loud gulping noise.

Flat, striped body

11 Its thin, oval-shaped body and vibrant colors make this regal fish stand out, even against the beautiful coral reefs it calls home. It often hides in rocky crevices between the corals.

Body color can change when the fish is hunting.

Bright red body during breeding season

12 Swimming at a speed of up to 68 mph (110 km/h), this fish herds smaller fish into densely packed "bait balls" to make them easier to attack. It slashes at the ball with its bill, then snaps up any fish that are stunned or wounded.

13 Watch out! This fish can shock its prey into submission. Its body stores power, which it can discharge when hunting or if it is attacked.

Long, cylindrical body

14 Most of the time, this fish swims in the open sea. When it is time to breed, it undertakes a huge journey, swimming up rivers to lay its eggs in fresh water.

TEST YOURSELF

STARTER

Ocean sunfish
Pygmy seahorse
Sockeye salmon
Royal angelfish
Sailfish

CHALLENGER

European plaice
Leopard moray eel
Tiger shovelnose catfish
Steephead parrotfish
Electric eel

GENIUS!

Atlantic footballfish
Oarfish
Arapaima
European sturgeon

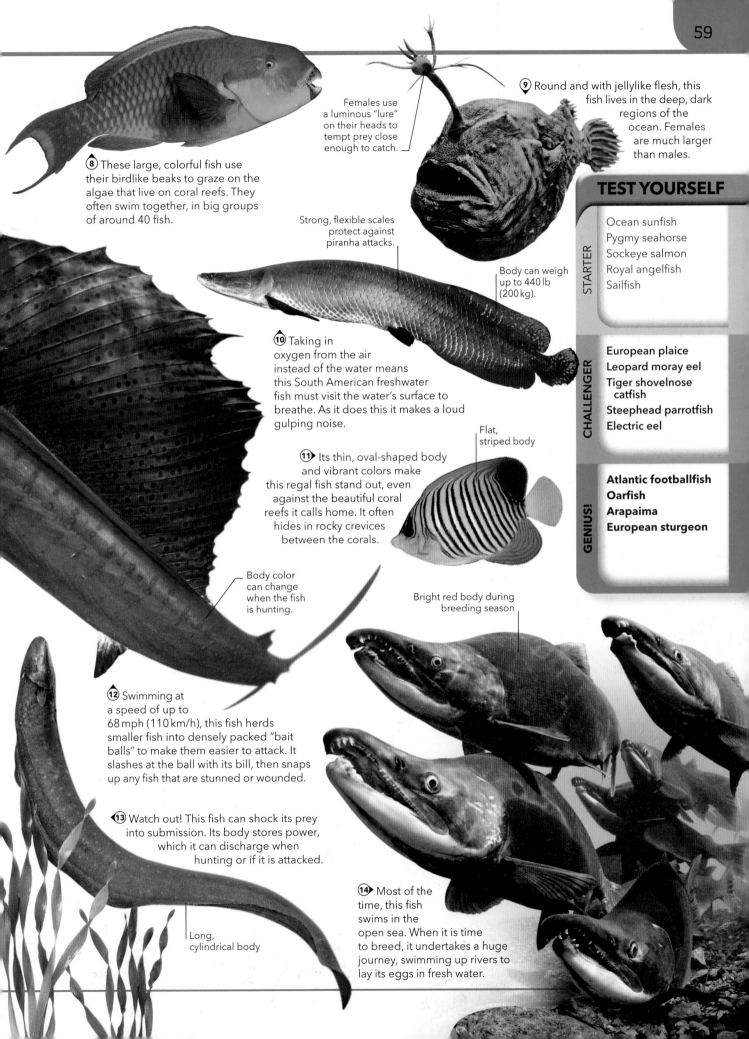

TEST YOURSELF

① This fish can grow big—up to 15 ft (4.5 m) long. It hunts near the bottom of the reef, searching for fish and squid, which it sucks into its mouth and swallows whole.

② These little fish live between the fronds of stinging sea anemones. Mucus on their skin protects them from being stung by their anemone host.

Yellow tips on the pectoral fins

③ Rough, bright-orange scales give this fish perfect camouflage against a coral reef. It is one of the most venomous fish in the world, with poisonous spines to put off any potential predators. It has a beard of seaweedlike strands that give it its name.

④ Caves and crevices are the perfect hiding places for this 9¾-ft- (3-m-) long fish. It waits until it can smell prey swimming past, then darts out, catching its meal with sharp, curved teeth.

Orange stripes across body

⑤ Strong teeth help this fish crunch its way through shellfish and sea urchins. If threatened, it can use its dorsal fin to wedge itself inside a hole, so that predators cannot pull it out.

Dorsal fin extends along the back.

Dorsal fin has a black patch at the top.

Enlarged scales above the base of the fin are used to produce sound.

⑥ Cruising smoothly across the reef, this predator hunts for small fish, crabs, and octopus. It can grow up to 5¼ ft (1.6 m) long and is often the biggest predator on the reef.

Reef rovers

Coral reefs are tropical havens, home to a vast variety of colorful ocean life. Each coral structure is made up of thousands of tiny animals called polyps. When a polyp dies, its rocky skeleton remains, and new polyps grow on top. Over time they build up, becoming coral reefs that provide food and shelter to thousands of animals.

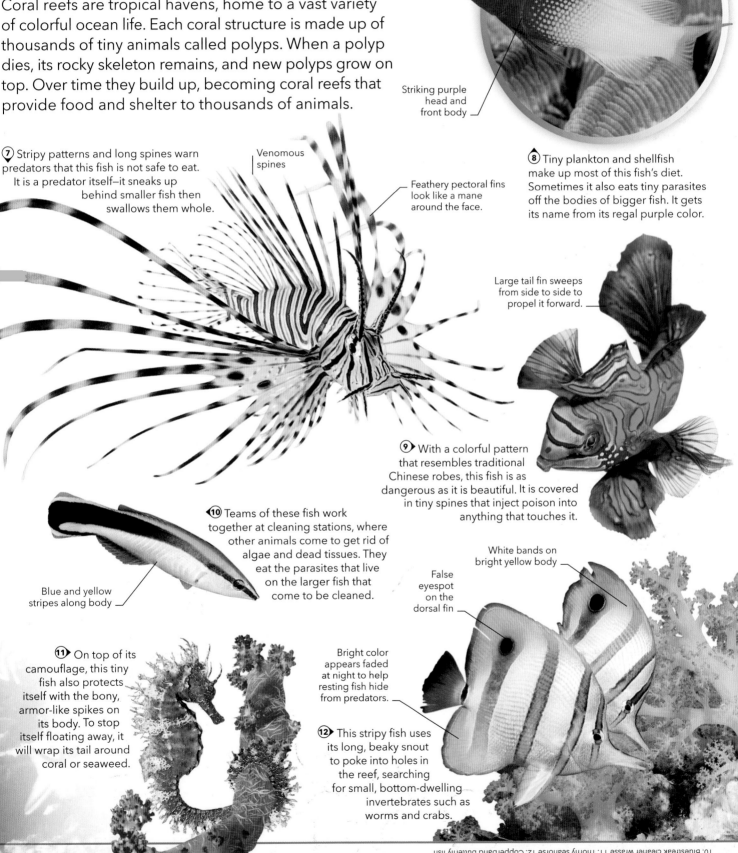

Striking purple head and front body

7 Stripy patterns and long spines warn predators that this fish is not safe to eat. It is a predator itself—it sneaks up behind smaller fish then swallows them whole.

Venomous spines

Feathery pectoral fins look like a mane around the face.

8 Tiny plankton and shellfish make up most of this fish's diet. Sometimes it also eats tiny parasites off the bodies of bigger fish. It gets its name from its regal purple color.

Large tail fin sweeps from side to side to propel it forward.

9 With a colorful pattern that resembles traditional Chinese robes, this fish is as dangerous as it is beautiful. It is covered in tiny spines that inject poison into anything that touches it.

10 Teams of these fish work together at cleaning stations, where other animals come to get rid of algae and dead tissues. They eat the parasites that live on the larger fish that come to be cleaned.

Blue and yellow stripes along body

White bands on bright yellow body

False eyespot on the dorsal fin

11 On top of its camouflage, this tiny fish also protects itself with the bony, armor-like spikes on its body. To stop itself floating away, it will wrap its tail around coral or seaweed.

Bright color appears faded at night to help resting fish hide from predators.

12 This stripy fish uses its long, beaky snout to poke into holes in the reef, searching for small, bottom-dwelling invertebrates such as worms and crabs.

ANSWERS: 1. Yellowfin grouper 2. Ocellaris clown fish 3. Tasseled scorpion fish 4. Giant moray 5. Orange-lined triggerfish 6. Blacktip reef shark 7. Lionfish 8. Royal gramma 9. Mandarin fish 10. Bluestreak cleaner wrasse 11. Thorny seahorse 12. Copperband butterfly fish

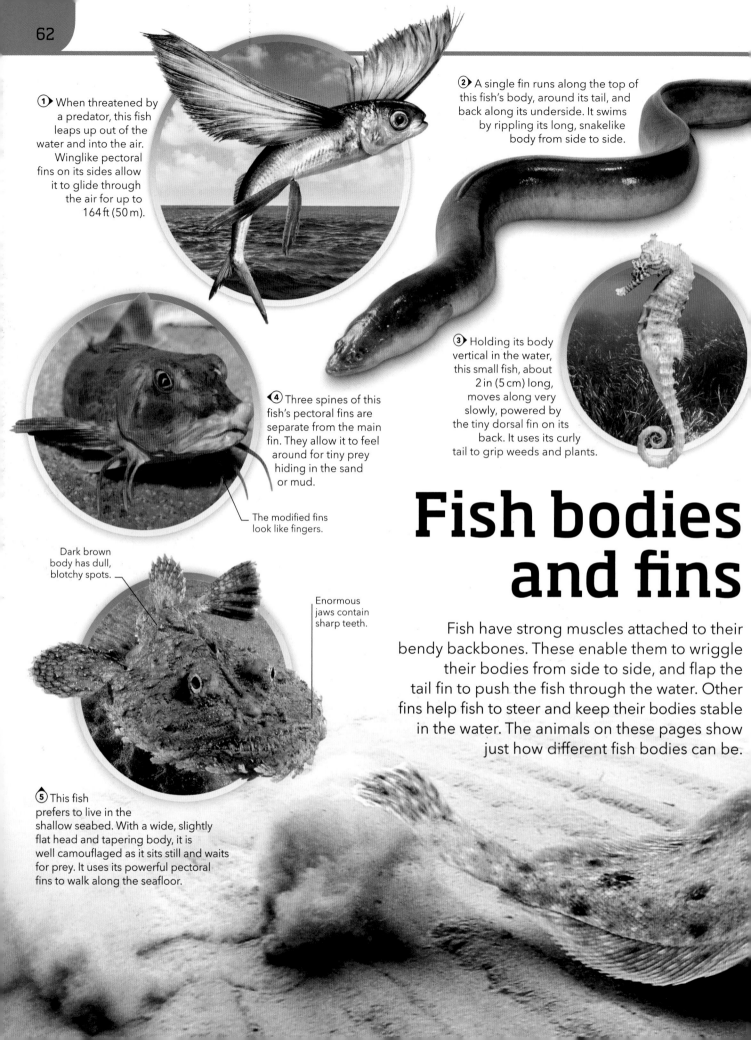

1 When threatened by a predator, this fish leaps up out of the water and into the air. Winglike pectoral fins on its sides allow it to glide through the air for up to 164 ft (50 m).

2 A single fin runs along the top of this fish's body, around its tail, and back along its underside. It swims by rippling its long, snakelike body from side to side.

4 Three spines of this fish's pectoral fins are separate from the main fin. They allow it to feel around for tiny prey hiding in the sand or mud.

The modified fins look like fingers.

3 Holding its body vertical in the water, this small fish, about 2 in (5 cm) long, moves along very slowly, powered by the tiny dorsal fin on its back. It uses its curly tail to grip weeds and plants.

Dark brown body has dull, blotchy spots.

Enormous jaws contain sharp teeth.

Fish bodies and fins

Fish have strong muscles attached to their bendy backbones. These enable them to wriggle their bodies from side to side, and flap the tail fin to push the fish through the water. Other fins help fish to steer and keep their bodies stable in the water. The animals on these pages show just how different fish bodies can be.

5 This fish prefers to live in the shallow seabed. With a wide, slightly flat head and tapering body, it is well camouflaged as it sits still and waits for prey. It uses its powerful pectoral fins to walk along the seafloor.

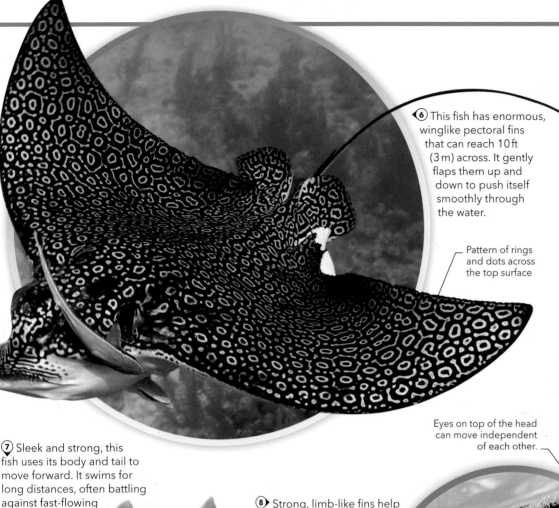

⑥ This fish has enormous, winglike pectoral fins that can reach 10 ft (3 m) across. It gently flaps them up and down to push itself smoothly through the water.

Pattern of rings and dots across the top surface

⑦ Sleek and strong, this fish uses its body and tail to move forward. It swims for long distances, often battling against fast-flowing water and river currents.

⑧ Strong, limb-like fins help this fish pull itself up and right out of the water. It hunts worms and insects in the mud, breathing in oxygen from water stored in pockets inside its gills.

Eyes on top of the head can move independent of each other.

Dark speckles on multi-colored, shiny body

Both eyes are on the same side of the body.

Young fish have black spots.

⑨ A solid, square-shaped body makes this fish a slow swimmer. It moves around by fluttering its fins. Since it cannot swim away fast enough, it releases a deadly toxin from its skin when threatened.

⑩ This fish has a flat, oval-shaped body. It swims by rippling its whole body up and down in wave motions that push it forward over the seabed.

ANSWERS: 1. Atlantic flying fish 2. European eel 3. Dwarf seahorse 4. Red gurnard 5. Shallow-water anglerfish 6. Spotted eagle ray 7. Rainbow trout 8. Blue-spotted mudskipper 9. Yellow boxfish 10. Southern flounder

4

AMPHIBIANS

Waiting to hatch

Amphibian eggs must stay wet while they develop. These tiny spotted salamanders are nearly ready to hatch. They already have eyes, tails, and gills—feathery organs on their necks, which will allow them to breathe underwater.

Amphibians

This group of animals can all breathe through their skin, which has to be kept moist at all times to absorb oxygen. As a result most amphibians live their whole lives in damp places. Some may also use organs called gills to breathe underwater, while others can develop lungs, which let them breathe air on land.

How to swim like a frog

01. Use your front legs and feet to make small movements, steering and controlling the direction of your body.

Tiny ponds
Some frogs carry their tadpoles on their backs to release them into pools of water collected in plants high in rainforest trees.

Suckers on the toes help the frog grip when on land.

Frogs cannot survive in salt water.

02. Stretch out as far as possible, then pull your front legs down to your sides.

Types of amphibians

Frogs and toads
This is the biggest amphibian group. These creatures have long, strong back legs and shorter front legs.

Newts and salamanders
These amphibians have lizard-like bodies, with long tails and four even-size limbs.

Caecilians
Wormlike and limbless, these amphibians are rarely seen. They live underground or underwater.

Gills are organs used to take in oxygen from the water.

Adult

Egg

Larva with four limbs

Larva with gill buds

Larva with two limbs

Salamander life cycle

Over its life, a salamander's body undergoes significant changes. It starts as an egg. The egg hatches into a larva in 19–50 days, which slowly develops gills, eventually becoming an adult in 2–5 months.

Webbed toes help the frog push through the water.

03. Kick hard with your powerful hind legs and use your webbed feet to push forward.

I don't believe it

The tadpole of the South American paradoxical frog is three times the size of the adult frog. It can be up to 10 in (25 cm) long, shrinking as it gets older.

Croaking

Male frogs and toads croak to attract females, and the louder they croak the more likely they are to succeed in finding a mate. Each species of frog and toad has its own unique croak.

Vocal sac inflates during croaking.

Deadly defenses

⚠ Found only in Colombia, the golden poison-dart frog is one of the most toxic animals on Earth. It stores its poison in its skin.

⚠ The tiny phantasmal poison frog only grows up to 1½ in (4 cm) in length, but still carries enough poison to kill a human.

⚠ Just touching the skin of the red-headed poison frog (below) would be enough to make you violently ill.

In numbers

60
The number of days a male Darwin's frog keeps tadpoles in his vocal sac after hatching. He then coughs up tiny frogs.

15 mph
(24 km/h) The maximum speed of the Andean salamander, the world's fastest amphibian.

6½ lb
(3 kg) The weight of a single adult goliath frog.

Biggest and smallest

6 ft (1.8 m)

6 ft (1.8 m)

The biggest of all amphibians is the colossal Chinese giant salamander. It lives in streams and rivers in central China.

¾ in (18mm) diameter

The tiniest amphibian is a frog, *Paedophryne amauensis*, from Papua New Guinea. Shown here on a US dime, it is ¼ in (7 mm) long.

Frogs and toads

With nearly 5,900 species, frogs and toads make up the biggest group of amphibians. These animals have wide mouths, eyes that stick out, and back legs used for leaping. There is no real scientific difference between frogs and toads, though most frogs have smoother, shinier skin.

Bright orange underside

1 This magnificently colored frog spreads its webbed feet to glide between the tops of trees in South American rainforests.

Silvery eyes with black markings

Bumpy skin

2 See-through skin means this frog's veins and organs are always on display. It is mainly active at night.

Babies are carried on the mother's back.

3 This well-camouflaged frog has a pointy nose and long eyelids, which look a little like horns.

Brown, ridged skin blends into the leaf litter on the forest floor.

5 Introduced to Australian sugarcane farms to eat insect pests, this toad spread so fast that it is now a pest itself.

4 The thick folds of skin over this patterned frog's eyes look a bit like horns. If threatened, it swells up and screams.

Huge mouth snatches prey such as mice, small birds, and other frogs.

Strands of large, yellow eggs

6 These European toads are very careful with their eggs—the male carries them around on his back until they hatch.

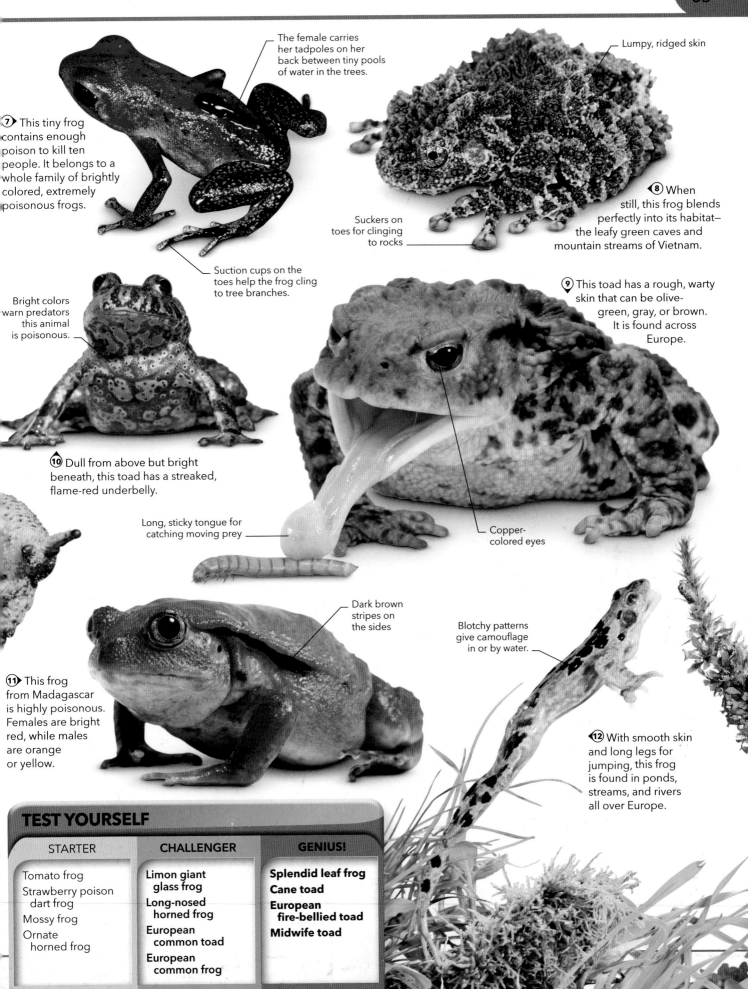

The female carries her tadpoles on her back between tiny pools of water in the trees.

Lumpy, ridged skin

7 This tiny frog contains enough poison to kill ten people. It belongs to a whole family of brightly colored, extremely poisonous frogs.

Suckers on toes for clinging to rocks

8 When still, this frog blends perfectly into its habitat— the leafy green caves and mountain streams of Vietnam.

Suction cups on the toes help the frog cling to tree branches.

Bright colors warn predators this animal is poisonous.

9 This toad has a rough, warty skin that can be olive-green, gray, or brown. It is found across Europe.

10 Dull from above but bright beneath, this toad has a streaked, flame-red underbelly.

Long, sticky tongue for catching moving prey

Copper-colored eyes

Dark brown stripes on the sides

Blotchy patterns give camouflage in or by water.

11 This frog from Madagascar is highly poisonous. Females are bright red, while males are orange or yellow.

12 With smooth skin and long legs for jumping, this frog is found in ponds, streams, and rivers all over Europe.

TEST YOURSELF

STARTER	CHALLENGER	GENIUS!
Tomato frog	Limon giant glass frog	Splendid leaf frog
Strawberry poison dart frog	Long-nosed horned frog	Cane toad
Mossy frog	European common toad	European fire-bellied toad
Ornate horned frog	European common frog	Midwife toad

Salamanders and newts

They look similar to lizards, but salamanders and newts are amphibians able to breathe through their thin skin. Some salamanders are even lungless and breathe only through their skin. A majority of salamanders live on land and return to the water only to breed. Newts are more aquatic than most salamanders.

Bright yellow-orange belly

1 This newt can be found across Europe. It is able to survive in very cold conditions and is usually found in mountainous areas.

2 An unusual hunter, this tropical, tree-living amphibian shoots its long tongue with a sticky tip to catch its prey.

Webbed feet help it swim.

Orange bumps show the position of poison-producing glands on the back.

Flat tail with blue markings

3 Named for a large reptile, this knobbly newt is found in parts of Asia. It has a prominent orange ridge on its spine.

Thin, wrinkled skin helps absorb oxygen.

4 This large, eellike creature has unusually tiny legs. It also has two rows of sharp teeth and a vicious, powerful bite.

Each leg has two toes.

5 This enormous salamander is the second-largest amphibian in the world, growing up to 4½ft (1.4m) long. It digests food slowly, and can go for weeks without eating.

6 Bright and beautiful, this salamander lives near mountain streams in eastern US. It often eats other salamanders.

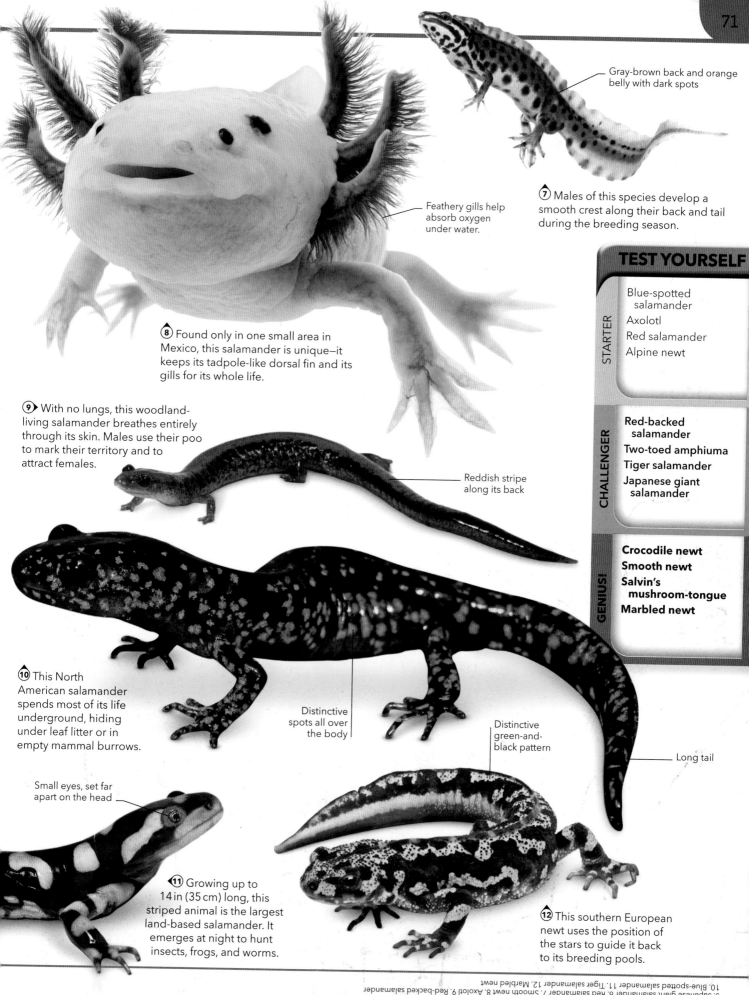

Gray-brown back and orange belly with dark spots

7 Males of this species develop a smooth crest along their back and tail during the breeding season.

Feathery gills help absorb oxygen under water.

8 Found only in one small area in Mexico, this salamander is unique—it keeps its tadpole-like dorsal fin and its gills for its whole life.

9 With no lungs, this woodland-living salamander breathes entirely through its skin. Males use their poo to mark their territory and to attract females.

Reddish stripe along its back

TEST YOURSELF

STARTER

- Blue-spotted salamander
- Axolotl
- Red salamander
- Alpine newt

CHALLENGER

- **Red-backed salamander**
- **Two-toed amphiuma**
- **Tiger salamander**
- **Japanese giant salamander**

GENIUS!

- **Crocodile newt**
- **Smooth newt**
- **Salvin's mushroom-tongue**
- **Marbled newt**

10 This North American salamander spends most of its life underground, hiding under leaf litter or in empty mammal burrows.

Distinctive spots all over the body

Distinctive green-and-black pattern

Long tail

Small eyes, set far apart on the head

11 Growing up to 14 in (35 cm) long, this striped animal is the largest land-based salamander. It emerges at night to hunt insects, frogs, and worms.

12 This southern European newt uses the position of the stars to guide it back to its breeding pools.

① Water is scarce in the areas where this African frog lives, and tadpoles are raised in puddles, rather than pools. The male watches over his tadpoles. If their puddle starts drying up, he digs a channel to one that is full of water, to top it up.

② When pairs of these frogs mate, they kick up a wet froth, into which the female lays her eggs. The spray dries with a hard crust, which protects the eggs and, later, the tadpoles.

③ Unlike most salamanders that lay their eggs in water, this species lays them in cool, damp, dark places on land. The female wraps herself tightly around her eggs until they hatch.

Tadpoles are almost high and dry—but the male is cutting a channel from a full puddle.

New life

Amphibians lay eggs that usually develop into aquatic tadpoles. The eggs must not dry out, so they are laid in water or damp places. Many amphibians lay eggs then leave, but some carefully watch over their young. Can you name these amphibian parents raising their young in lots of different ways?

The red underside of the tail contrasts with the darker color on top.

⑤ Wet Indian jungles are the habitat of a frog whose eggs develop right into tiny froglets, without ever going through a tadpole stage.

④ This amphibian attaches its eggs to the faces of rocks, twigs, or leaves in the water. Groups of females lay their eggs in the same place, creating huge clumps of them.

Soft, damp moss holds the eggs.

ANSWERS: 1. African bullfrog 2. Gray foam-nest tree frog 3. Strinati's cave salamander 4. Northern spectacled salamander 5. Amboli bush frog 6. Common frog 7. Common toad 8. Eyelash marsupial frog 9. Red-eyed tree frog 10. Ringed caecilian

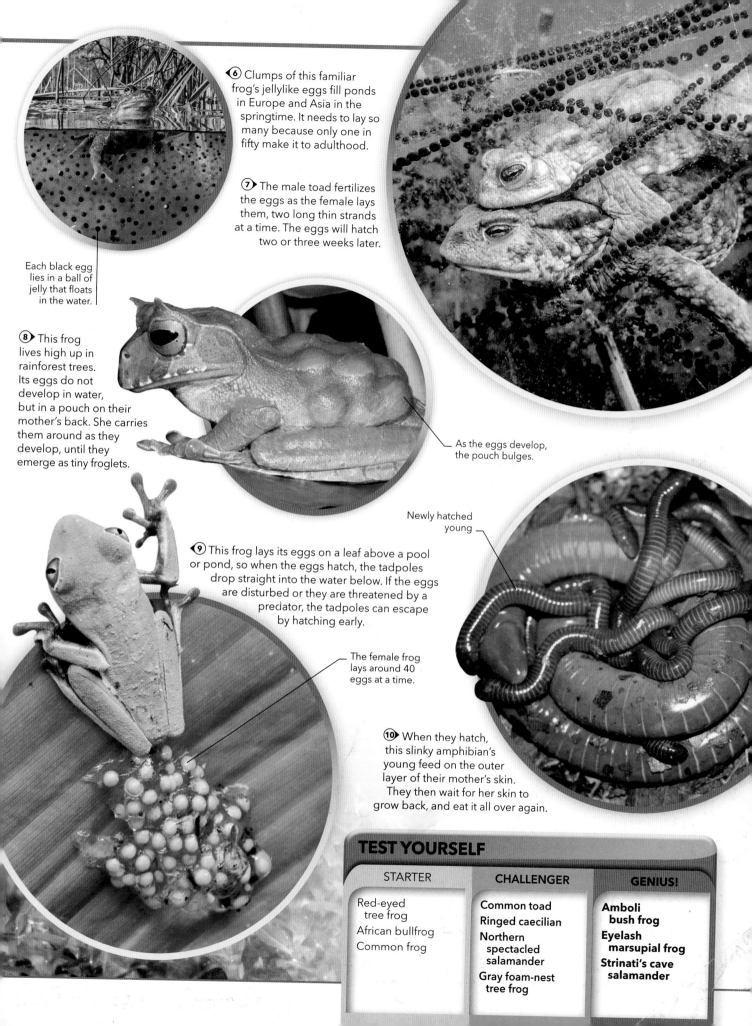

6 Clumps of this familiar frog's jellylike eggs fill ponds in Europe and Asia in the springtime. It needs to lay so many because only one in fifty make it to adulthood.

7 The male toad fertilizes the eggs as the female lays them, two long thin strands at a time. The eggs will hatch two or three weeks later.

Each black egg lies in a ball of jelly that floats in the water.

8 This frog lives high up in rainforest trees. Its eggs do not develop in water, but in a pouch on their mother's back. She carries them around as they develop, until they emerge as tiny froglets.

As the eggs develop, the pouch bulges.

9 This frog lays its eggs on a leaf above a pool or pond, so when the eggs hatch, the tadpoles drop straight into the water below. If the eggs are disturbed or they are threatened by a predator, the tadpoles can escape by hatching early.

Newly hatched young

The female frog lays around 40 eggs at a time.

10 When they hatch, this slinky amphibian's young feed on the outer layer of their mother's skin. They then wait for her skin to grow back, and eat it all over again.

TEST YOURSELF

STARTER	CHALLENGER	GENIUS!
Red-eyed tree frog	Common toad	Amboli bush frog
African bullfrog	Ringed caecilian	Eyelash marsupial frog
Common frog	Northern spectacled salamander	Strinati's cave salamander
	Gray foam-nest tree frog	

5 REPTILES

Vipers in hiding
The patterns on the scales of these Gaboon vipers allow them to blend in with dead leaves on the rainforest floor. There are at least seven snakes in this photograph—look for their pale heads with tiny black marks on the sides to find them.

Reptiles

Cold-blooded and scaly-skinned, reptiles have existed for hundreds of millions of years—even before the dinosaurs! Most of them lay eggs to reproduce, though a few snakes and lizards give birth to live young. Reptiles are found on land and in water all over the world, except for in the very coldest places.

Types of reptiles

Lizards and snakes
This is the biggest reptile group. It includes legless snakes, worm-like amphisbaenians, and lizards, which mostly have four legs.

Turtles and tortoises
These reptiles have tough protective shells attached to their skeletons. Turtles live in water and tortoises on land.

Crocodilians
This group includes the largest of the reptiles. They are powerful predators with long, strong, tooth-filled jaws.

Tuataras
Most members of this group lived alongside the dinosaurs. Only one species survives today, found in New Zealand.

01. Balance yourself well on a branch with the help of your unique Y-shaped feet.

A chameleon's tongue moves twice as fast as the fastest sports car.

03. Once you have spotted something, shoot your tongue out to catch it. Your sticky saliva will help secure your prey.

How to hunt like a chameleon

02. Stay as still as you can, looking for tasty insects. If you need to move, do it slowly so your prey does not notice.

Egg layers
Nearly all reptiles lay eggs, which hatch into miniature versions of their parents. A few, however, give birth to live young.

Homegrown hideaway

Tortoises are slow—running away would not get them very far. Instead, they carry a place of safety around with them at all times. If danger threatens, they retreat, hiding inside their shell.

Head stays as still as possible, to avoid detection by prey.

Head, legs, and tail can all be tucked safely away inside the shell.

Tongue shoots out at incredible speeds of up to 4,900 ft/sec (1,500 m/sec).

04. Pull your tongue back into your mouth. You will need to catch up to 20 insects every day to keep well nourished.

Biggest and smallest reptiles

The largest reptile of all is the saltwater crocodile, which lives in Oceania and Asia.

The Madagascan chameleon is the tiniest reptile. It is about the size of a sunflower seed.

⅞ in (21.6 mm)

6 ft (1.8 m)

21 ft (6.5 m)

Basking

Reptiles are cold-blooded, which means that their body temperature changes with the temperature outside. To keep themselves warm, they sunbathe, often on top of a nice warm rock. This behavior is called basking. To cool off they retreat into the shade.

Scales take in heat from the sun.

In numbers

3,000
The number of teeth a crocodile grows and loses during its lifetime.

22 mph
(35 km/h) The maximum speed of a saltwater crocodile on land.

34 ft
(10.4 m) The length of the longest anaconda snake.

10 ft
(3 m) The distance a spitting cobra can propel its venom into its prey's face and eyes.

Making an escape

Some lizards can break off their tails, to distract a predator while they run away. They then grow a new tail, which takes around 60 days.

End of the tail keeps moving even after it has detached.

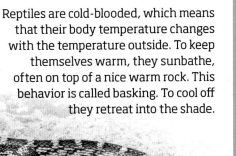

I don't believe it

Geckos can walk upside down across ceilings—their footpads have hairlike structures that form a sticky pad and help them stick to any surface they choose.

Distinctive line of short, raised spines down the center of the shell

Wormlike growth lures prey inside its powerful jaws.

2 Watch your toes! This reptile hides in the muddy bottoms of North American ponds or streams, waiting for prey to swim past.

1 Sometimes this animal's shell has yellow lines across it, which can join to create a messy web pattern. It enjoys sunbathing on logs high above the water's surface.

3 This reptile has a smooth, leathery shell—it does not have the same hard "scutes," or bony scales of its relatives.

Tubelike nostrils let it breathe above the surface, while hiding its body under water.

4 This South American reptile is very hard to spot on the muddy beds of rivers or lakes. Its shell is often covered with algae, giving it another level of disguise.

TEST YOURSELF

STARTER
- Aldabra giant tortoise
- Green sea turtle
- Leatherback sea turtle
- Pancake tortoise

CHALLENGER
- Alligator snapping turtle
- Common snake-necked turtle
- False map turtle
- Big-headed turtle

GENIUS!
- Chinese soft-shelled turtle
- Indian starred tortoise
- Red-eared slider
- Matamata

Pointed humps on shell

5 This beautifully patterned creature lives in southern Asia, where its stripes camouflage it in the dry grass. It mainly eats plants, fruit, and flowers.

Triangular head looks like leaves or bark floating in the water.

6 Originally from North America, this reptile is often kept as a pet. Escaped or released pets have found their way into ponds, lakes, and rivers across the world.

Red stripe behind the eye

Flat, light shell allows it to move faster than most others in its family.

7 This reptile's shell can be gray, black, or a mixture of colors. It only comes ashore once a year, to lay eggs on the beach it was born on.

8 An unusually flat, flexible shell allows this African reptile to squeeze itself into narrow crevices to hide.

9 This Asian reptile has a head so big that it cannot pull it inside its shell. It also has an extremely long tail.

10 With a neck half as long as its shell, this Australian animal must bend its head sideways to pull it back into the safety of its shell.

Turtles and tortoises

These reptiles have a protective shell on their back, and they all lay eggs. Some turtles stay in water for almost their entire lives—they only visit land to lay their eggs. Can you tell a land-living tortoise from a water-loving turtle?

Webbed feet and claws

Growth rings on the domed shell show the animal's age.

Thick, tough skin stretches across this turtle's back instead of hard scutes.

11 This enormous reptile is around 3½ ft (1.1 m) long and can weigh as much as 550 lb (250 kg). It is named for an island in the Seychelles.

12 Up to 7¼ ft (2.2 m) long, this huge animal travels vast distances in the ocean—as much as 10,000 miles (16,000 km) a year. Jellyfish are one of its favorite meals.

The tail helps grip when climbing.

Its eyes can rotate independently of each other.

Males become more colorful during the breeding season.

② This lizard lives on rocky shores of the Galápagos Islands, where it feeds on seaweeds. Some even dive down to graze at the bottom of the sea.

① Famous for its ability to change color, this technicolor lizard lives high up in thick Madagascan forest trees.

Sharp claws help it cling to slippery, seaweed-covered rocks.

Lots of lizards

Forming the biggest group of reptiles, with more than 5,500 species, lizards come in all shapes and sizes—from tiny geckos to the 10-ft- (3-m-) long Komodo dragon. These scaly, cold-blooded animals are found on every continent except Antarctica.

Black stripe across the eye

③ Only the strongest males of this small species are bright blue in color. Females, the young, and weaker males are green or brown.

Sticky pads under its toes cling to smooth surfaces.

④ When threatened, this creature puffs up its body to make itself look bigger, while also sticking out its tongue and hissing.

Sharp spikes

Folds of skin on the neck help regulate body temperature.

⑤ This large animal is a common sight in trees across South America. It uses its sharp teeth to feast on fruit and leaves.

The long tail makes up two-thirds of its body length.

6 The biggest lizard of all, this huge reptile is found only on a few small islands in Indonesia. Sailors once mistook it for a mythical beast.

7 This flame-red creature is shier than its colors suggest. It spends much of its time hiding in burrows.

The tail can detach when a predator attacks.

The forked tongue is flicked out and can detect food from as far as 3 miles (5 km) away.

8 This venomous North American lizard has a fearsome reputation of crushing its prey to death.

"Armored" skin with small, strong scales

9 Found only in the rainforests of a large East African island, this lizard can drink nectar from flowers.

Sharp claws on its feet help dig burrows.

Large, strong toe pads for grip

The tail is held upright when walking.

10 Small and spiky, this creature lives in dry desert areas in central Australia.

11 This vibrant reptile lives in North America. It can change color, but is not a chameleon.

The pink throat pouch is used to attract mates.

Fan of skin opens up when the lizard opens its mouth wide.

12 If a flash of its wide neck ruff is not enough to put off a predator, this lizard makes a run for it, sometimes rising up on to two legs.

TEST YOURSELF

STARTER	CHALLENGER	GENIUS!
Panther chameleon	**Marine iguana**	**Madagascar day gecko**
Green iguana	**Frilled lizard**	**Green anole**
Blue-tongued skink	**Thorny devil**	**Fire skink**
Turquoise dwarf gecko	**Komodo dragon**	**Gila monster**

1 This brightly colored creature lives in rainforest trees. Its slender, muscular body allows it to hunt geckos and skinks easily.

Powerful jaw muscles

Brown coloring helps camouflage in muddy waters.

2 Reaching up to 33 ft (10 m) long, this Asian snake gets its name from the netlike, criss-cross patterns all over its body.

Its wide body is covered with V-shape markings.

3 This venomous snake lives all over Africa. When threatened, it puffs up its body and makes a loud hissing noise.

4 At more than 150 lb (70 kg), this South American snake is the heaviest in the world. It can kill by squeezing prey, such as deer, in its coils.

5 One bite from this Australian black-headed snake contains enough venom to kill 100 humans. It can grow up to 8 ft (2.5 m) long.

The defensive, S-shaped pose shows that it is ready to strike.

7 This creature's scales, patterned with black rings and blotches, have an iridescent sheen.

The hood opens when the animal feels threatened.

6 This Asian serpent has venom powerful enough to kill humans, but it mainly preys on mice and rats.

Dark circles or "eyespots" on the back

TEST YOURSELF

STARTER	CHALLENGER	GENIUS!
Indian cobra	**Western diamond-backed rattlesnake**	**Bush viper**
Yellow-lipped sea krait	**Giant anaconda**	**Inland taipan**
Vine snake	**Rainbow boa**	**Green tree python**
Puff adder	**Central American coral snake**	**Reticulated python**

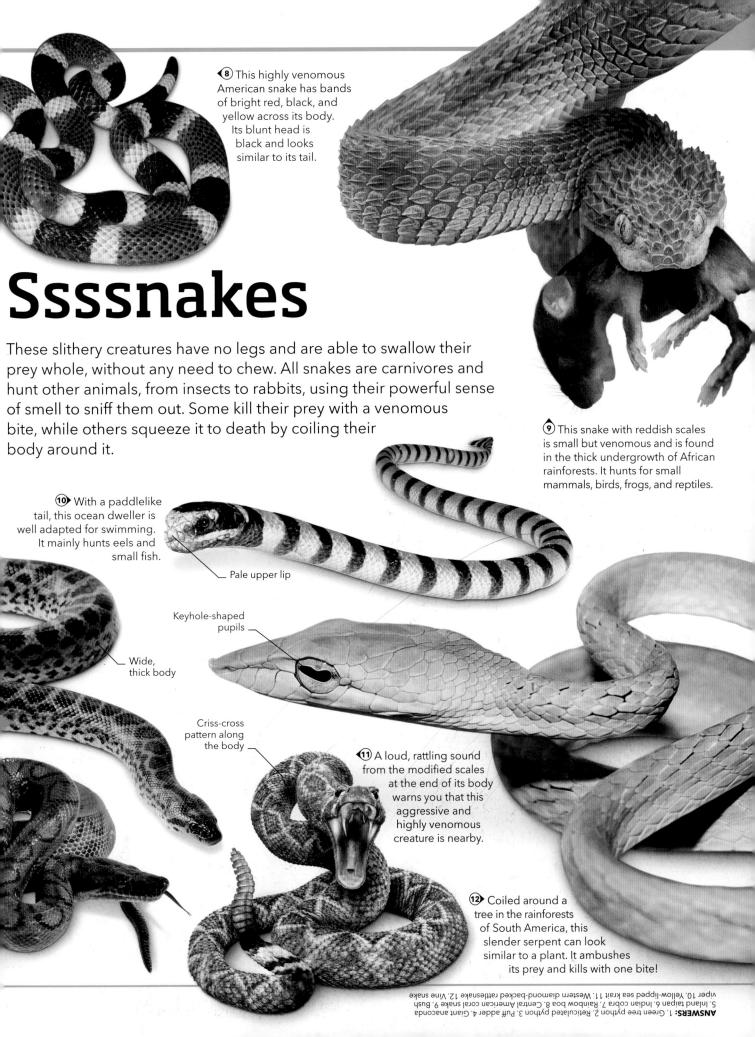

8 This highly venomous American snake has bands of bright red, black, and yellow across its body. Its blunt head is black and looks similar to its tail.

Ssssnakes

These slithery creatures have no legs and are able to swallow their prey whole, without any need to chew. All snakes are carnivores and hunt other animals, from insects to rabbits, using their powerful sense of smell to sniff them out. Some kill their prey with a venomous bite, while others squeeze it to death by coiling their body around it.

9 This snake with reddish scales is small but venomous and is found in the thick undergrowth of African rainforests. It hunts for small mammals, birds, frogs, and reptiles.

10 With a paddlelike tail, this ocean dweller is well adapted for swimming. It mainly hunts eels and small fish.

Pale upper lip

Keyhole-shaped pupils

Wide, thick body

Criss-cross pattern along the body

11 A loud, rattling sound from the modified scales at the end of its body warns you that this aggressive and highly venomous creature is nearby.

12 Coiled around a tree in the rainforests of South America, this slender serpent can look similar to a plant. It ambushes its prey and kills with one bite!

ANSWERS: 1. Green tree python 2. Reticulated python 3. Puff adder 4. Giant anaconda 5. Inland taipan 6. Indian cobra 7. Rainbow boa 8. Central American coral snake 9. Bush viper 10. Yellow-lipped sea krait 11. Western diamond-backed rattlesnake 12. Vine snake

Scaly stories

Reptiles have tough, waterproof skin that stops moisture from escaping, enabling them to live in dry places. On top of the skin is a protective layer of small, hard plates called scales, which protects the skin from damage and parasites. Scales come in a huge variety of shapes, sizes, and colors.

① Modified scales form tiny hornlike spines across this lizard's body, making it rough and spiky. Combined with brown blotches, they camouflage it well. When threatened, it puffs up its spiny body.

Small, smooth scales fill the spaces between the spines.

② Small, evenly sized scales cover the body of this small lizard. These are covered with markings that look like the spots on a big cat's fur.

The scales look smooth and polished.

③ Even, flat, and polished scales protect the skin of this slithering reptile. It is sleek and slender, with rows of small, dark spots or blotches running down its back.

The pattern on each animal's shell is unique.

④ The top of this North American animal's shell is plain dark green while the underside is bright red with artistic, swirling patterns.

5 In low light, this snake looks brown or black. When the light bounces off of it, however, its scales glimmer with rainbow colors.

Skin is covered by tough, waterproof scales

6 Bony plates called scutes fuse together to form a hard shell on the back of this African reptile. Each scute is marked with a starlike pattern.

7 This freshwater predator's body is covered with bony plates that act as protective armor. Its underside is covered with scales that are smoother and smaller, and more uniform in pattern, than those on its back and tail.

8 Small, bumpy, and unevenly sized scales cover this lizard. It has special cells underneath its skin that allow it to change color when it is excited or needs to hide.

9 At the tip of this creature's tail is a ring of hollow scales that knock against each other to make a rattling sound as a warning not to come any closer!

Black spots all over its body

10 Tough, pointed scales stop this snake's skin from getting scratched by tree branches. It is named for the spiky, raised scales above its eyes.

Each scale has a ridge down its center.

11 Pointed, leaf-shaped scales give this African snake a bristly, spiky look. It slithers through the undergrowth hunting for frogs, birds, and mice.

TEST YOURSELF

STARTER	CHALLENGER	GENIUS!
Mugger crocodile	**Sunbeam snake**	**Coast horned lizard**
Jeweled chameleon	**Smooth snake**	**Painted turtle**
Mojave rattlesnake	**Radiated tortoise**	**Spiny bush viper**
Leopard gecko	**Eyelash viper**	

Short, blunt snout

Teeth are constantly replaced as they wear out.

① This is the smallest crocodile species—the biggest adults reach around 4 ft (1.2 m) in length. It lives in streams and swamps in the forests of western Africa.

Skin is a mixture of brown, gray, and yellow.

② The heavy ridge above this caiman's eyes makes it look like it's wearing a pair of glasses. It is the most common crocodilian of all.

Gray or olive skin

Raised scales on the tail help it swim fast.

③ A unique fish-eating species from India, this animal has a long, thin snout it sweeps left and right through the water to catch prey, which it then swallows whole.

Large scales with bony cores

④ Named after a river in Africa, this crocodile is usually found sunning itself on river banks, or floating like a log.

Mouth is often held open to lose heat on hot days.

Make it snappy

Crocodiles, alligators, and their close relatives form a group called the crocodilians—powerful predators, with rows of sharp teeth in their long jaws. Alligators usually have rounded, U-shaped snouts while crocodiles have longer, V-shaped ones, with the lower teeth clearly visible even when their mouths are closed.

⑤ This is the world's biggest reptile—up to 20 ft (6 m) long. It is the only crocodilian frequently seen out at sea and is a fearsome predator, attacking any animal it can catch.

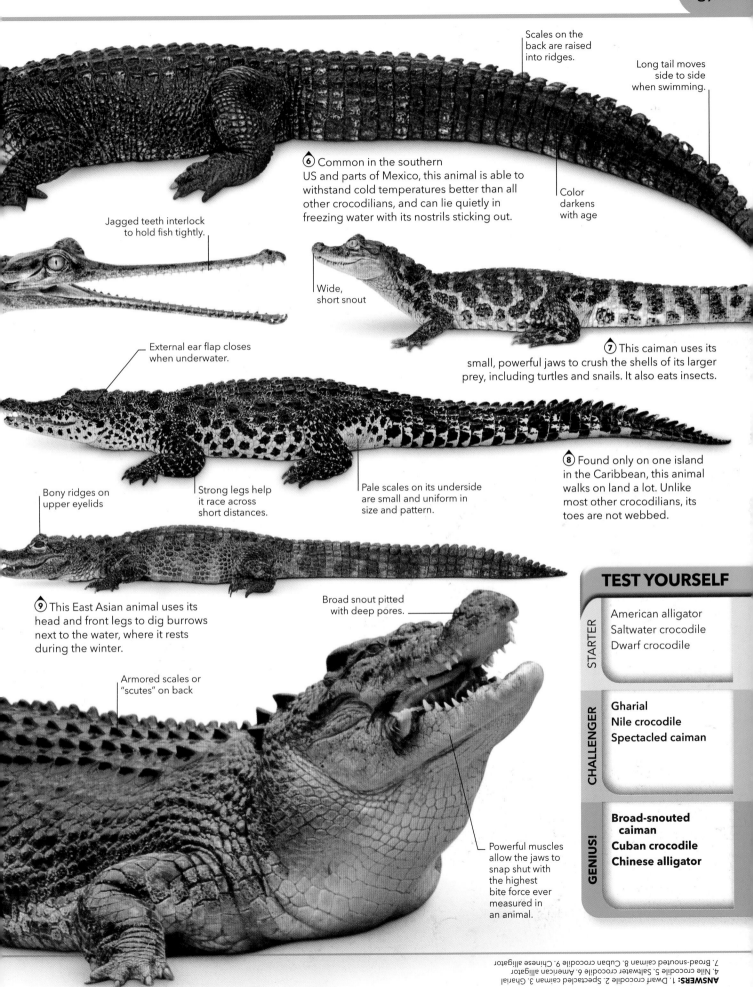

Scales on the back are raised into ridges.

Long tail moves side to side when swimming.

⑥ Common in the southern US and parts of Mexico, this animal is able to withstand cold temperatures better than all other crocodilians, and can lie quietly in freezing water with its nostrils sticking out.

Color darkens with age

Jagged teeth interlock to hold fish tightly.

Wide, short snout

⑦ This caiman uses its small, powerful jaws to crush the shells of its larger prey, including turtles and snails. It also eats insects.

External ear flap closes when underwater.

⑧ Found only on one island in the Caribbean, this animal walks on land a lot. Unlike most other crocodilians, its toes are not webbed.

Bony ridges on upper eyelids

Strong legs help it race across short distances.

Pale scales on its underside are small and uniform in size and pattern.

⑨ This East Asian animal uses its head and front legs to dig burrows next to the water, where it rests during the winter.

Broad snout pitted with deep pores.

Armored scales or "scutes" on back

Powerful muscles allow the jaws to snap shut with the highest bite force ever measured in an animal.

TEST YOURSELF

STARTER
American alligator
Saltwater crocodile
Dwarf crocodile

CHALLENGER
Gharial
Nile crocodile
Spectacled caiman

GENIUS!
Broad-snouted caiman
Cuban crocodile
Chinese alligator

ANSWERS: 1. Dwarf crocodile 2. Spectacled caiman 3. Gharial 4. Nile crocodile 5. Saltwater crocodile 6. American alligator 7. Broad-snouted caiman 8. Cuban crocodile 9. Chinese alligator

6

BIRDS

Flamingo flock

Many birds live alone for much of the year, while others prefer to live in pairs or small groups. Some gather in flocks, like these flamingos, which may also form huge breeding colonies of more than one million birds. This protects them from predators that could steal their eggs and chicks.

What is a bird?

Birds are warm-blooded, lay eggs, and have feathers. They are vertebrates, with especially light, air-filled bones. Most birds are able to fly.

Beak for catching and holding food

All birds have wings, although not all of them can fly. The wings flap with great force to lift the bird off the ground.

Feathers keep birds warm and enable most of them to fly.

Bird claws and feet vary depending on their lifestyle.

Birds

Looking at birds today, it may be hard to believe that they are related to dinosaurs. The earliest birds emerged around 150 million years ago, and today there are more than 10,000 species across 28 different major groups. They vary from tiny hummingbirds, which can be as small as a bee, to ostriches that are 10 ft (3 m) tall.

Types of birds

Perching birds
More than half of all bird species are in this group, also called the passerines. They have sharp-clawed feet that are adapted for perching.

Non-perching birds
This group is divided into many smaller ones, covering a huge range of birds. They include owls, parrots, birds of prey, penguins, and flamingos.

Red-crowned cranes often stay with one partner for their whole lives.

How to court like a crane

01. Choose your partner carefully so your courtship dance is both graceful and in perfect time.

02. Move toward your partner, spreading your wings and leaping gracefully.

Storing food

This lizard has been impaled on a thorn.

The red-backed shrike hunts small animals, including insects, lizards, and mice. It stores food for later by impaling its catch on thorny branches.

The acorn woodpecker drills a series of holes into tree bark. It then fills each hole with an acorn, building up a store of food for it to eat in the winter months.

In numbers

620 miles
(1,000 km) The distance that a wandering albatross can fly in a single day.

6,000
The number of nests in a single tree built by one red-billed quelea colony.

1,854 ft
(565 m) The maximum depth an emperor penguin can dive to.

Seabirds

Some birds, such as these gannets, spend most of their time at sea. They only visit land to raise their young. Gannets are experts at fishing and can reach depths of up to 98 ft (30 m) to catch prey.

I don't believe it

Owls can't chew, so they swallow small prey, such as mice, whole. They then cough up pellets of undigested body parts including fur and bones.

Migration

Around 4,000 species of birds regularly migrate, flying between their summer breeding grounds and winter feeding areas.

The bar-tailed godwit migrates almost 9,320 miles (15,000 km) from Alaska to New Zealand, without stopping to feed on the way.

Arctic terns migrate to the Antarctic and back every year. Over a lifetime of almost 30 years, this bird can fly a distance of up to 1½ million miles (2.4 million km).

03. Once close to your partner, tip your head back and call loudly to each other.

Sneaky bird

Cuckoos lay their eggs in other birds' nests. Once hatched, the cuckoo chick pushes any other eggs out, and is fed by the other chicks' parents.

04. Bow to each other and then dance around your partner, and bounce up and down together.

05. Remember the dance routine—you may perform it many times together to demonstrate your strong bond.

Bony crest, called a casque, may perhaps help protect the head as the bird runs through thick forest.

① Along with other members of its family, this is the national bird of New Zealand. Growing up to 25 in (65 cm) long, this small bird has fur-like plumage.

Short, bare neck

② Growing up to 6¼ ft (1.9 m), this is the largest bird in Australia. It can survive for several days without food or water.

Long bill with nostrils for sniffing out worms.

④ About 5 ft (1.5 m) tall, this bird lives in Australia and Papua New Guinea. Its name comes from two Papuan words: *kasu*, which means "horned," and *wari*, which means "head."

Reddish brown feathers

③ Unlike most other ratites, this South American ground-living bird can fly but prefers to run away from danger.

Bare skin

Wings raised for balance when running

Chicks have stripes for camouflage.

Plumage can be light gray or brown.

⑤ At around 4 ft (1.2 m) tall and weighing up to 88 lb (40 kg), this is the largest bird in South America. The male mates with many females and then builds one nest where he looks after his eggs from all the females.

The long, thin crest curls upwards.

⑥ This graceful bird nests and sleeps on the ground. It takes regular dust baths to keep its feathers clean.

Color of the bright double wattle may change when the bird is excited.

Yellowish brown, speckled feathers

TEST YOURSELF

STARTER	CHALLENGER	GENIUS!
Ostrich	**Southern cassowary**	**Southern brown kiwi**
Emu	**Lesser rhea**	**Elegant crested tinamou**
Greater rhea	**Gray tinamou**	**Red-winged tinamou**
	Little spotted kiwi	**Northern cassowary**

Grounded!

Ostriches and their relatives make up a group of birds called ratites. These birds have wings but they are short, with small wing muscles, which means most ratites are unable to fly. This does not necessarily slow them down—ostriches can run faster than most horses can gallop, reaching speeds of up to 43 mph (70 km/h).

⑦ The smallest bird in its family, this New Zealand native is smaller than the average chicken, and has speckled feathers.

Feathers look like shaggy fur.

Stiff tail feathers are rattled to warn off predators.

Long neck almost bare of feathers

Gray plumage

⑧ A ground-living, ground-nesting bird from South America, it can fly, but only for short distances.

⑨ This speedy bird runs with its wings folded and its head stuck out. It is able to swim, which is useful when it needs to cross rivers, as it cannot fly. This sociable animal lives in groups of up to 30 birds, and is smaller than its other close relative.

Single wattle

⑪ Shy and solitary, this single-wattled bird lives in northern parts of New Guinea. Its dark feathers help it hide in thick vegetation in swamps and forests.

⑩ The biggest bird on Earth, and the fastest on land, the males of this species can be up to 9 ft (3 m) tall. Their eggs are enormous, too—equal in size to about 24 chicken eggs.

Long, muscular legs help it run fast.

Two toes

Strong three-toed feet, for jumping and kicking out if attacked.

1 At around 18 in (47 cm) tall, this is a large bird of the North American prairies. Males display to females by inflating the bright orange air sacs on their necks and making snapping noises with their tails.

2 Originally from Asia, this bird has been introduced all over the world for hunting. Males are brightly colored, while the females are brown and speckled.

Red patch around the eyes

3 To survive in the Arctic, this bird has white plumage for camouflage in winter, and grows rock-gray feathers in the summer.

Snow white winter plumage

4 The males of this species perform complicated courtship dances, making strange noises including clicks, gurgles, and pops. The bird gets its name from a Gaelic word that means "horse of the forest."

Curly, feathered crest

White spot on shoulder

Males fan out tail feathers when displaying for females.

5 This bird is very well camouflaged in the coniferous forests where it lives. If a predator is nearby it freezes, only flying off at the last possible moment.

Females have a reddish brown plumage.

7 This little bird is hunted in the wild but is also farmed, both for its meat and for its tiny eggs.

Bright red comb above the eyes

Striped crown

6 Large but secretive, this bird lives in the rainforests of Central America. Unlike its mostly ground-feeding relatives, it feeds on fruit and insects in the treetops.

Game birds

This group of birds has long been hunted by humans, for food or for sport. Most of them spend their lives on the ground, taking to the skies only to escape from danger. Can you tell a quail from a capercaillie, or a grouse from a jungle fowl?

Males have a bright red flap of skin called a wattle.

8 The colorful males of this species are known for their amazing displays—they fan out their tails and then strut in front of the females.

Tail feathers have green-and-blue "eyes."

9 Originally from North America, this noisy bird is farmed all over the world. During their courtship display, males raise their feathers, fan their tails, and make gobbling sounds.

10 This gray bird makes a noisy whirring noise if it is flushed into the air. It prefers to spend its time on the ground.

Brick-red face

Dark patch on belly

11 The ancestor of the domestic chicken, this colorful bird lives in large flocks in the forests of Asia.

Males have a large crest

Powerful legs help dig mounds for building nests.

12 This chicken-size, Australian bird lives in a habitat with dense, low-growing eucalyptus trees. It makes its nest out of warm, rotting vegetation.

ANSWERS: 1. Greater prairie chicken **2.** Common pheasant **3.** Rock ptarmigan **4.** Western capercaillie **5.** Spruce grouse **6.** Great curassow **7.** Common quail **8.** Indian peafowl **9.** Wild turkey **10.** Gray partridge **11.** Red jungle fowl **12.** Malleefowl

① A small, colorful bird from the eastern parts of Australia, this broad-tailed parrot has a bright red head with white cheeks.

Blue tail and wings

② The largest flying parrot, this bright blue South American bird can grow up to 3 ft (1 m) long.

Its massive beak is adapted for cracking nuts.

Parrot parade

These gorgeous parrots are not just pretty faces—they are also among the most intelligent birds. Most parrots are sociable birds who enjoy living together in big flocks, and some species form long-term pair bonds with their partners. However, many of them are endangered because they are caught and sold as pets.

③ Named after royalty, this parrot reigns in Australian deserts. It constantly keeps moving in search of seeds, fruit, and insects.

Pale green shoulders

④ Native to Africa, this highly intelligent parrot is skilled in copying human speech and mimicking sounds. Its slate-gray body ends in a bright red tail.

⑤ This brainy, colorful bird can grow up to 5½ in (14 cm) long and live for up to 30 years. It feeds on flower nectar and pollen.

Thin flight feathers

⑥ This slow and flightless nocturnal bird from New Zealand walks for long distances every night, looking for nuts, fruit, bark, moss, and leaves. It is today critically endangered.

⑦ A common bird in Australia, this brightly colored pink-and-gray parrot nests in holes in trees.

Large feet relative to the size of its body

⑧ The males and females of this unusual parrot species look completely different. The females are red and blue, like this one, but males are green.

ANSWERS: 1. Eastern rosella 2. Hyacinth macaw 3. Princess parrot 4. Congo African gray parrot 5. Rainbow lorikeet 6. Kakapo 7. Galah 8. Eclectus parrot 9. Ring-necked parakeet 10. Scarlet macaw 11. Kea 12. Parakeet 13. Sulfur-crested cockatoo 14. Rosy-faced lovebird 15. Olive-headed lorikeet

9 ▶ Originally from India, this little green parrot is now found in many cities across Europe. It is recognized by the distinctive marking on its throat.

10 ▶ Possibly the most easily recognized of all parrots, this bird is red, yellow, and blue, but named for just one of those colors. Growing up to 35 in (90 cm) long, this is a huge bird.

Blue flight feathers give way to red tail feathers.

11 ▶ This unusual bird has a loud, screeching call. It is the world's only mountain-living parrot, and eats rotting meat as part of its diet.

Red patch under wing

Barred, yellow head

12 ▶ One of the world's most familiar parrots, this Australian bird is a swift flier. It lives in flocks that can range from a few to thousands of birds.

The long blue tail has a black underside.

Bright yellow crest is raised when the bird is threatened.

13 This noisy bird is quite popular as a pet. When a flock feeds on the ground, one bird sits in a tree nearby, to watch out for predators.

14 ◀ Small and pink-faced, this African parrot gathers in small groups. Pairs sleep close together, side-by-side, with their heads resting on each other.

White plumage except on its head and tail

15 ▶ This bird is only found on the island of Timor in Southeast Asia. The color on its head contrasts with the bright green collar on its neck.

TEST YOURSELF

STARTER	CHALLENGER	GENIUS!
Parakeet	**Olive-headed lorikeet**	**Galah**
Hyacinth macaw	**Congo African gray parrot**	**Eclectus parrot**
Sulfur-crested cockatoo	**Princess parrot**	**Kakapo**
Rosy-faced lovebird	**Ring-necked parakeet**	**Kea**
Scarlet macaw		**Eastern rosella**
Rainbow lorikeet		

Flight

A bird's body is designed for flight. Most have light, air-filled bones; super-strong chest muscles to power their wings; and streamlined, feather-covered bodies. Other animals, including many insects, take to the air, but none have the skill, stamina, and speed of these expert fliers.

In numbers

21,120 ft
(6,437 m) The height above sea level at which a bar-headed goose can fly.

47 mph
(76 km/h) A common swift's speed in level flight—the fastest recorded speed of any bird.

200 mph
(320 km/h) The speed at which a peregrine falcon can dive.

I don't believe it

As they fly over the African savanna, flocks of more than 1.5 billion red-billed quelea are a constant threat to farmers. This bird can be so destructive that it is sometimes called the "feathered locust."

Types of feathers

Down feather
These fine, fluffy feathers are found closest to the bird's body. They trap a layer of air, keeping the bird warm.

Contour feather
These small feathers cover the bird's body. They overlap each other, making the bird smooth and streamlined.

Flight feather
Long and strong, these feathers are found in the tail and along the edges of the wings. They help power the bird through the air.

How to hover like a hummingbird

01. Find a bright, nectar-filled flower that you would like to sip from, then fly over it so that it is within easy reach of your beak.

02. Using your unique wing joints, twist your wings vertically to fly up. Twist them horizontally again to drive you forward.

Flying patterns

Birds do not all fly through the air in the same way. Some beat their wings in a repeated, steady pattern. Others glide through the air, hardly moving their wings, or combine gliding and flapping.

Fast flapping: Birds with small wings and heavy bodies, such as ducks, beat their wings fast and regularly.

Intermittent flapping: Some birds, including woodpeckers, move between gliding and periods of fast flapping.

Slow flapping: Slow, leisurely wingbeats are used by birds with fairly large wings, such as gulls.

Random flapping: When hunting insects, birds such as swallows dart around with a mix of gliding and flapping.

Flying as one

Before they settle down for the night, huge groups of common starlings fly in a display called a murmuration. They move through the air, changing direction in unison as they go, creating swirling patterns in the sky. Flying in flocks like these is usually a defensive move against predators.

Common starling

03. Flap your wings really fast so you hover in the air in the same spot while you enjoy the delicious nectar.

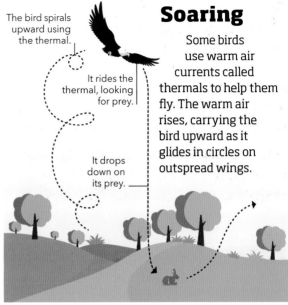

The bird spirals upward using the thermal.

It rides the thermal, looking for prey.

It drops down on its prey.

Soaring

Some birds use warm air currents called thermals to help them fly. The warm air rises, carrying the bird upward as it glides in circles on outspread wings.

Types of wings

Speed
Tapered, pointed wings allow some birds, such as this common swift, to move through the air at incredible speeds. This wing type allows it to twist and turn, as it hunts for insects on the wing.

Direction
Rounded wings help birds, such as jays, fly nimbly between trees in densely forested areas. This wing shape gives birds the ability to quickly change direction mid-flight.

Hovering
Birds with short, triangular wings, such as hummingbirds, can flap them very quickly—more than 20 times a second. This enables them to hover in a fixed spot for a long time.

Gliding
Long, slender wings allow birds, including albatrosses, to glide over long distances. Once airborne, this bird may not need to flap its wings for hours as it glides over oceans.

1 Deft at drilling holes in trees, this woodpecker drinks the sap that flows out, and also preys on any insects that come to drink the sap. It is recognized by its striking red head and chest.

Its bill can be up to 7½ in (19 cm) long.

Its bill is long enough to take eggs from nests in tree holes.

2 Brightly colored and enormous, this bird's beak is the largest, relative to body size, of all birds. Although the beak looks heavy, it is hollow and light, with tiny, criss-crossing struts to strengthen it.

3 This bird's favorite food is fruit, but it also eats eggs and small animals such as lizards, insects, and other birds. While its beak comes in different colors, it can be recognized by its white chest and a blue patch around its eyes.

Toucans and woodpeckers

These beaky birds are perfectly adapted for living in trees. Toucans use their long, light beaks to reach fruit from trees, or to poke into tree holes to pull out prey. Woodpeckers use their strong beaks to hammer into bark, drilling out any insects hiding within.

Large claws with a powerful grip

4 The colored underwings of this bird flash as it flaps its wings in flight. It lives in North America.

Males have red, mustache-like markings on the face.

5 Often heard before it is seen, this bright European bird has a loud, laughing call.

Black patch around eye

Long tongue reaches deep into ant hills to lap up the insects inside.

6 Oak trees are both home and a source of food for this bird. Using its sharp beak, it stores nuts in tiny holes it makes or finds in tree bark.

White underparts with black streaks

Blue patch below the eyes

Flexible tail can be folded to touch the head.

Short, rounded wings are only used for brief flights.

7 Dull in color at birth, this Central American bird takes on a bright, jewel-green color as it becomes an adult. This makes it almost impossible to spot among the leaves of the tropical forests.

8 At around 21 in (55 cm) long, this bird has a striking red crown. It drills into dead wood to find insects to eat, while its stiff tail feathers help it balance.

Barb-like bristles around the beak

Jagged edges on beak are helpful for picking and eating fruit.

9 At about 13 in (32 cm) long, this is the largest bird in its family. It is found at altitudes of up to 9,842 ft (3,000 m) in South and Southeast Asia.

10 This bird has a bright yellow and red breast with a black horizontal band running through the middle. It eats fruit mostly, but will also catch small prey such as insects and lizards.

TEST YOURSELF

STARTER	CHALLENGER	GENIUS!
Toco toucan	**Northern flicker**	**Collared aracari**
Green woodpecker	**Red-breasted sapsucker**	**Acorn woodpecker**
White-throated toucan	**Black woodpecker**	**Great barbet**
	Emerald toucanet	

ANSWERS: 1. Red-breasted sapsucker 2. Toco toucan 3. White-throated toucan 4. Northern flicker 5. Green woodpecker 6. Acorn woodpecker 7. Emerald toucanet 8. Black woodpecker 9. Great barbet 10. Collared aracari

2 One of the rare owls that can be spotted in broad daylight, this bird has a well-rounded head, large yellow eyes, and no visible "ears."

3 This enormous bird is known to hunt large animals that it then pulls apart with its beak, like the big bird of prey it is named after.

Feathery ear tufts

1 Whitish feathers sit like long ear tufts above this owl's eyes and nose. When disturbed or agitated, it stretches its body to its full height and raises the tufts as a sign of warning.

Feathers protect the legs from attack by prey.

Night owls

These beautiful birds are the ultimate nighttime hunters. Owls have excellent hearing and can see well in the dark. Their eyes are so big that they cannot move–instead, the owl turns its whole head, with the help of its flexible neck. Owl wings are fringed with soft feathers that enable them to fly almost silently. They can be almost on top of their prey before being noticed.

4 A good digger, this bird lives in holes in treeless grassland. It is also happy using any existing den, or even human-made structures. Unlike most owls, it is also active during the day.

Long legs help with digging in the ground.

5 Perfectly camouflaged for its icy Arctic habitat, this owl is expert at picking off small mammals hidden under the snow.

Heavy black barring on females; males are whiter.

6 This owl was named after its distinctive "mo-poke" call. Usually heard rather than seen, this is the smallest owl in Australia, with adults growing up to only 13½ in (35 cm).

7 The light circles around this tropical owl's eyes make it look a little like it is wearing a pair of glasses.

Small black blotches on white flight feathers

Wingspan reaches up to 6½ ft (2 m).

Heart-shaped face helps push sounds into ears.

8 Only 5½ in (14 cm), this is the world's smallest owl—about the same size as a sparrow, or even a tiny fairy creature! Its slanting "eyebrows" over large tawny eyes make it easy to recognize.

9 This bird is found on all continents except Antarctica. It hunts in open countrysides, and can be seen nesting in farm buildings.

10 Named after its color, this streaky brown owl is found in several shades, including reddish brown and gray-brown.

11 This owl is named after the spiky feather tufts on its head. At 23½ in (60 cm) long, it is the largest owl found in the Americas.

The round, gray-and-white face is surrounded by a circle of feathers, and is the largest in all owls.

Short, striped tail feathers

12 At about 27½ in (70 cm), this owl is huge. It lives in the northern parts of Europe and North America. Its thick layer of gray feathers keeps it warm and camouflaged in these cold climates.

TEST YOURSELF

STARTER
Barn owl
Snowy owl
Tawny owl
Great gray owl

CHALLENGER
Eagle owl
Crested owl
Spectacled owl
Elf owl

GENIUS!
Great horned owl
Burrowing owl
Boobook owl
Short-eared owl

ANSWERS: 1. Crested owl 2. Short-eared owl 3. Eagle owl 4. Burrowing owl 5. Snowy owl 6. Boobook owl 7. Spectacled owl 8. Elf owl 9. Barn owl 10. Tawny owl 11. Great horned owl 12. Great gray owl

① Unusually for a bird of prey, this bird eats mostly fruit, from one particular type of tree. It uses its hooked beak to tear through the fruit's tough skin.

Short, rounded wings help it fly between trees.

② This forest hunter is found across Europe and parts of Asia. It hides in a tree or bush, waiting for small birds to appear. It then darts out to snatch its prey from the air or ground.

Wingspan of up to 6½ ft (2 m)

Pure white underside

Fish caught in talons

③ While it mainly hunts for fish, this bird will eat whatever it can find, including frogs, small birds, and carrion. Pairs of birds sometimes hunt together.

White head

Wide wings with fingerlike tips

④ A famous face—this is the national bird of the US. It mainly hunts fish, using its sharp, curved claws to snatch them out of the water.

Wingspan can be up to 7½ ft (2.3 m) long.

Red facial skin

⑤ This African bird is named after the French word for an acrobat because of the way it rocks from side to side as it flies. It hunts for long hours each day, looking for mice or birds.

Short tail is almost hidden by wings when sitting.

Tuft of feathers looks like a beard.

⑥ Also known as the bearded vulture, this unusual scavenger eats mostly bones. Sometimes it carries a bone into the sky, then drops it down onto rocks, smashing the bone open to get to the tasty marrow inside.

Long tail feathers

Birds of prey

With razor-sharp claws and hooked beaks, birds of prey—or raptors—are top predators. Most of them hunt live prey, taking to the skies to look for mice, frogs, fish, or other birds to eat. Some are scavengers and feed on carrion—the remains of dead animals.

⑦ A shrill "klee!" call lets you know that this small North American falcon is overhead. It has black sideburn-like bands on the sides of the face, and tends to bob its tail when perched.

⑧ Circling low over land, this bird with an owllike face searches for small animal prey. It has especially good hearing, and can hear tiny movements below. This graceful flier has a jet plane named after it!

Chestnut back with black flecks

White feathers indicate that these are young birds.

⑨ One of the largest raptors, weighing more than 13 lb (6 kg), this bird is named after its shiny yellow-brown crown feathers. It hunts everything from reptiles and small mammals to fish.

Fanned tail helps the bird slow down before impact.

Narrow wings tucked into the body when diving

Pale blue beak

Crest of dark feathers

⑩ Unlike most other falcons, this bird stays on the ground, strutting around on its long legs, rooting for food. It eats carrion as well as small animals, and even insects it digs up with its flat claws.

⑪ This animal is a prime scavenger. It uses its sharp, hooked beak to tear open tough flesh. Treated like royalty, it gets first pick of any carrion, even if it was found by other birds!

Fleshy, orange growth above its beak

⑫ In a technique called "stooping," this superb hunter plummets down at incredible speeds of up to 200 mph (322 km/h) and catches its prey in mid-air, making it the fastest bird on earth.

Band of black feathers across the wing edges

TEST YOURSELF

STARTER
Bald eagle
Peregrine falcon
White-bellied sea eagle
Golden eagle

CHALLENGER
Palm-nut vulture
Northern harrier
American kestrel
King vulture

GENIUS!
Lammergeier
Bateleur
Crested caracara
Eurasian sparrowhawk

Whose beak?

Most birds eat a particular food, such as seeds, insects, or fish. Their beaks, or bills, are clever tools, as their shapes make eating that food as easy as possible. Here are some super-specialized beaks—can you figure out whose is whose?

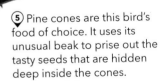

1 Rough, jagged edges make this long, reddish bill perfect for holding on to slippery fish. The bird gets its name from its rust-colored chest.

2 Sweeping its head from side-to-side as it wades through the water, this bird uses its long bill to sift out tiny animals.

3 Once this bird of prey has caught its meal, it uses its sharp, hooked beak to strip the meat from the bones, and tear it into small pieces.

Wide, rounded end

Long, slender beak

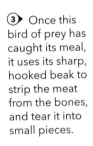

4 This red bird uses its sharp, curved bill to pierce through the flower's base to reach the nectar instead of dipping into it. It also eats small insects.

5 Pine cones are this bird's food of choice. It uses its unusual beak to prise out the tasty seeds that are hidden deep inside the cones.

6 This tiny bird has a long, straight beak that is perfectly shaped to fit tube-shaped flowers. It hovers in front of them and sips at the sugary nectar inside.

The tips of the beak cross over.

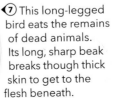

7 This long-legged bird eats the remains of dead animals. Its long, sharp beak breaks though thick skin to get to the flesh beneath.

ANSWERS: 1. Red-breasted merganser 2. Eurasian spoonbill 3. Golden eagle 4. Crimson sunbird 5. Crossbill 6. Anna's hummingbird 7. Marabou stork 8. Wreathed hornbill 9. European nightjar 10. Gouldian finch 11. American avocet 12. European robin 13. Great white pelican 14. Atlantic puffin

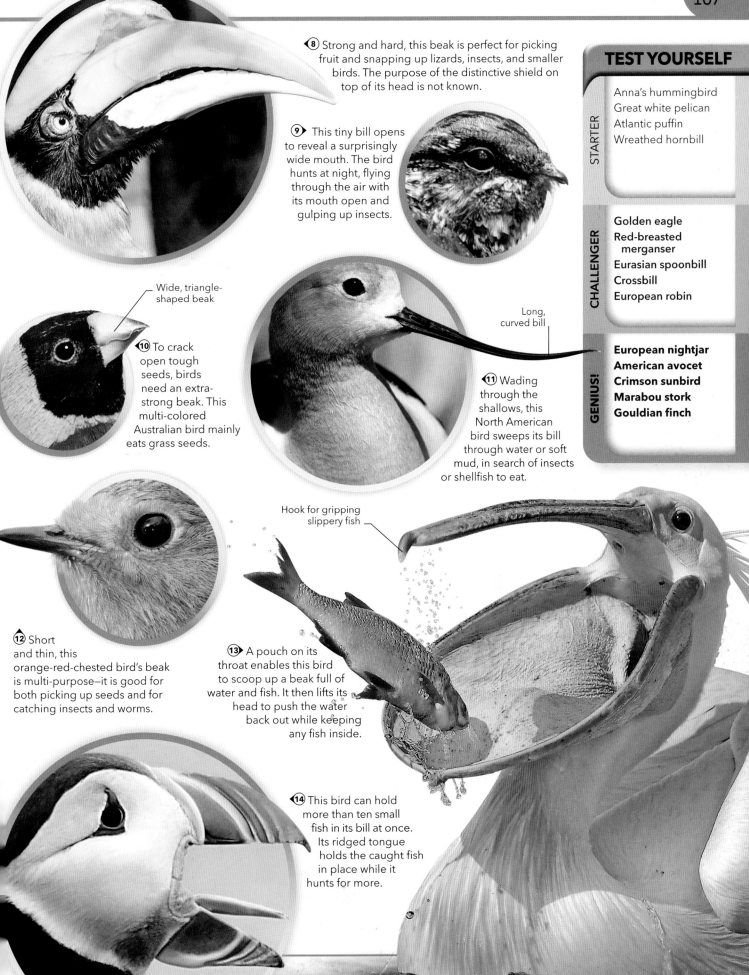

8 Strong and hard, this beak is perfect for picking fruit and snapping up lizards, insects, and smaller birds. The purpose of the distinctive shield on top of its head is not known.

9 This tiny bill opens to reveal a surprisingly wide mouth. The bird hunts at night, flying through the air with its mouth open and gulping up insects.

Wide, triangle-shaped beak

10 To crack open tough seeds, birds need an extra-strong beak. This multi-colored Australian bird mainly eats grass seeds.

Long, curved bill

11 Wading through the shallows, this North American bird sweeps its bill through water or soft mud, in search of insects or shellfish to eat.

Hook for gripping slippery fish

12 Short and thin, this orange-red-chested bird's beak is multi-purpose—it is good for both picking up seeds and for catching insects and worms.

13 A pouch on its throat enables this bird to scoop up a beak full of water and fish. It then lifts its head to push the water back out while keeping any fish inside.

14 This bird can hold more than ten small fish in its bill at once. Its ridged tongue holds the caught fish in place while it hunts for more.

Broad, white chin strap

1 One of the best known birds in North America, it often gathers in big, noisy flocks. It eats roots, grass, and seeds.

Paler upper breast

Large, spatula-shaped bill

2 Seen throughout North America, Europe, and Asia, this bird uses its unique bill to filter tiny animals and seeds out of the water to eat.

4 This bird can be found on fresh water all over Asia, Europe, and North America. Males have a green head and females are streaky-brown all over.

3 Usually seen in pairs, this bird spends most of its life along the coastline. If threatened, its young will dive into the water to escape.

Males have a protruding knob on the red bill.

Orange "sails" are used for display.

Males have orange cheek plumes.

Ducks and geese

These birds are strong swimmers and spend their whole lives on or near water. Their webbed feet propel them across the surface of the water, and glands near their tails produce oil to keep their feathers waterproof. Powerful fliers, some species migrate long distances to breed.

5 Originally from Asia, the male of this bird has stunning plumage. Females are less colorful, with gray heads, brown backs, and white circles around the eyes.

Males have a spotted chest.

6 Long, pointed claws enable this bird to perch in trees. Males have a band of color around their necks.

Males have a longer plume of black feathers on the back of the head than females.

7 This elegant, red-billed bird usually stays with the same partner its whole life. The pair will reuse the same nest every year and care for their young together.

8 The black tip on its bill, bright yellow eyes, and plume make this bird stand out. It feeds on plants and small animals by diving under the water.

ANSWERS: 1. Canada goose 2. Northern shoveler 3. Common shelduck 4. Mallard 5. Mandarin duck 6. Ringed teal 7. Black swan 8. Tufted duck 9. King eider 10. Wood duck 11. Graylag goose 12. Smew 13. Whooper swan

Curly tail feathers

Purple-blue wing patch

9) Found across the Arctic, this bird breeds on the coasts of Alaska, Canada, and Greenland. The male has bright colors around its bill.

Pale blue crown

Pinkish brown breast

Dark feathers with pale fringes

Males have a red eye-ring.

10) Tree holes are the perfect nesting place for this bird. It feeds by filtering water through its beak, or searches for acorns and berries on land.

11) Big and bulky, this bird weighs up to 7¼ lb (3.3 kg). It has a sharp, honking call and usually stays in large, noisy flocks.

Pink feet

Crest lies flat when bird is in flight.

Males have a distinctive black-and-white coloring.

12) This shy and uncommon bird breeds by lakes and rivers. Males and females both have crests, but otherwise look quite different. The female is gray with a dark brown head.

Yellow bill with black tip and edges

13) Very strong fliers, these birds travel hundreds of miles on their annual migration. They do this in large flocks, making loud, honking calls to each other while in flight.

Strong 7¾ ft (2.35 m) wide wings allow this bird to glide on the wind.

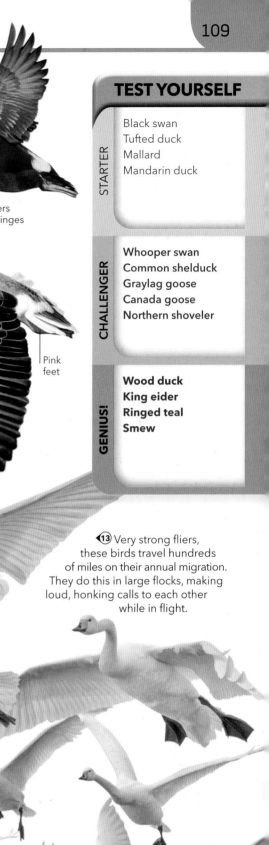

TEST YOURSELF

STARTER

Black swan
Tufted duck
Mallard
Mandarin duck

CHALLENGER

Whooper swan
Common shelduck
Graylag goose
Canada goose
Northern shoveler

GENIUS!

Wood duck
King eider
Ringed teal
Smew

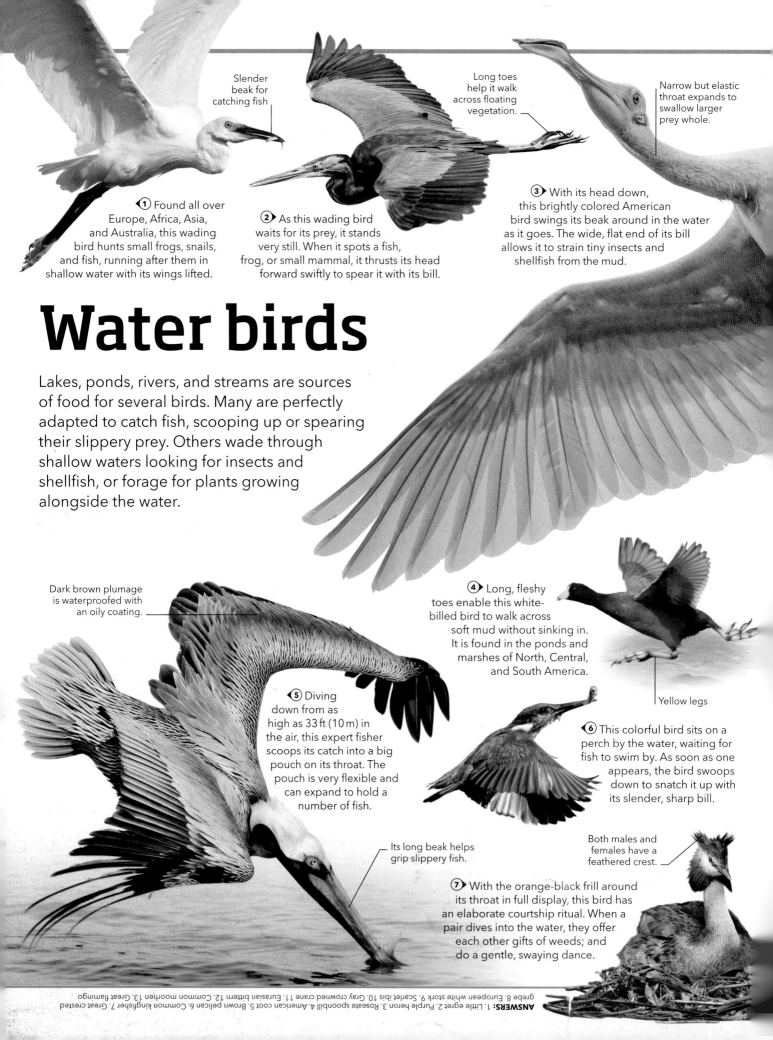

Slender beak for catching fish

Long toes help it walk across floating vegetation.

Narrow but elastic throat expands to swallow larger prey whole.

① Found all over Europe, Africa, Asia, and Australia, this wading bird hunts small frogs, snails, and fish, running after them in shallow water with its wings lifted.

② As this wading bird waits for its prey, it stands very still. When it spots a fish, frog, or small mammal, it thrusts its head forward swiftly to spear it with its bill.

③ With its head down, this brightly colored American bird swings its beak around in the water as it goes. The wide, flat end of its bill allows it to strain tiny insects and shellfish from the mud.

Water birds

Lakes, ponds, rivers, and streams are sources of food for several birds. Many are perfectly adapted to catch fish, scooping up or spearing their slippery prey. Others wade through shallow waters looking for insects and shellfish, or forage for plants growing alongside the water.

Dark brown plumage is waterproofed with an oily coating.

④ Long, fleshy toes enable this white-billed bird to walk across soft mud without sinking in. It is found in the ponds and marshes of North, Central, and South America.

Yellow legs

⑤ Diving down from as high as 33 ft (10 m) in the air, this expert fisher scoops its catch into a big pouch on its throat. The pouch is very flexible and can expand to hold a number of fish.

⑥ This colorful bird sits on a perch by the water, waiting for fish to swim by. As soon as one appears, the bird swoops down to snatch it up with its slender, sharp bill.

Its long beak helps grip slippery fish.

Both males and females have a feathered crest.

⑦ With the orange-black frill around its throat in full display, this bird has an elaborate courtship ritual. When a pair dives into the water, they offer each other gifts of weeds; and do a gentle, swaying dance.

ANSWERS: 1. Little egret 2. Purple heron 3. Roseate spoonbill 4. American coot 5. Brown pelican 6. Common kingfisher 7. Great crested grebe 8. European white stork 9. Scarlet ibis 10. Gray crowned crane 11. Eurasian bittern 12. Common moorhen 13. Great flamingo

The long, narrow bill clatters when it communicates.

8 ▶ Found in Africa and Europe, this bird eats small frogs, rodents, and grasshoppers. It builds big, bulky nests in trees or high up on buildings in cities.

Its sensitive bill is used to search for food in the mud.

Red wattle under chin

Stiff, golden crown of feathers on the head

9 ▶ The national bird of Trinidad, this tropical wader gets its bright red color from the tiny shellfish it eats.

Black-tipped wings

Long toes spread the bird's weight on soft mud.

10 ▶ This African bird forages for seeds, insects, and lizards on the ground. It courts a mate by leaping into the air, flapping its wings, and bowing its head.

The broad, angled bill sifts food from the surface of the water.

11 ◀ Streaky feathers are the perfect camouflage for this bird, which lives in reed beds. Often heard during the mating season, its call sounds like a loud "boom"!

12 ▼ With large yellow feet and a yellow-tipped red beak, this bird is a familiar sight in wetlands and even cities all over the world.

13 ▶ Wading in shallow water in large flocks, this bird can be up to 5 ft (1.5 m) tall. To feed on insects and shrimps, it lowers its exceptionally long neck and turns its head upside down.

Long legs allow it to search for food in deeper water.

TEST YOURSELF

STARTER	CHALLENGER	GENIUS!
Greater flamingo	Great crested grebe	Purple heron
Common kingfisher	Common moorhen	American coot
Brown pelican	Gray crowned crane	Eurasian bittern
Scarlet ibis	European white stork	Little egret
Roseate spoonbill		

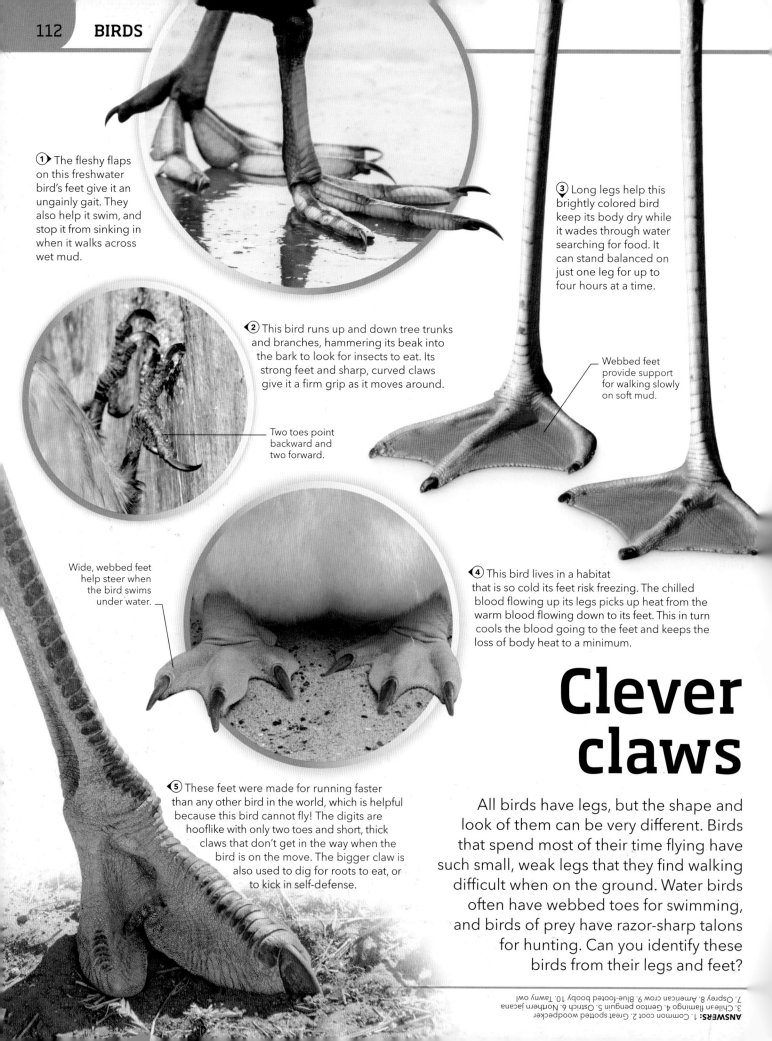

1 The fleshy flaps on this freshwater bird's feet give it an ungainly gait. They also help it swim, and stop it from sinking in when it walks across wet mud.

3 Long legs help this brightly colored bird keep its body dry while it wades through water searching for food. It can stand balanced on just one leg for up to four hours at a time.

2 This bird runs up and down tree trunks and branches, hammering its beak into the bark to look for insects to eat. Its strong feet and sharp, curved claws give it a firm grip as it moves around.

Webbed feet provide support for walking slowly on soft mud.

Two toes point backward and two forward.

Wide, webbed feet help steer when the bird swims under water.

4 This bird lives in a habitat that is so cold its feet risk freezing. The chilled blood flowing up its legs picks up heat from the warm blood flowing down to its feet. This in turn cools the blood going to the feet and keeps the loss of body heat to a minimum.

5 These feet were made for running faster than any other bird in the world, which is helpful because this bird cannot fly! The digits are hooflike with only two toes and short, thick claws that don't get in the way when the bird is on the move. The bigger claw is also used to dig for roots to eat, or to kick in self-defense.

Clever claws

All birds have legs, but the shape and look of them can be very different. Birds that spend most of their time flying have such small, weak legs that they find walking difficult when on the ground. Water birds often have webbed toes for swimming, and birds of prey have razor-sharp talons for hunting. Can you identify these birds from their legs and feet?

ANSWERS: 1. Common coot 2. Great spotted woodpecker 3. Chilean flamingo 4. Gentoo penguin 5. Ostrich 6. Northern jacana 7. Osprey 8. American crow 9. Blue-footed booby 10. Tawny owl

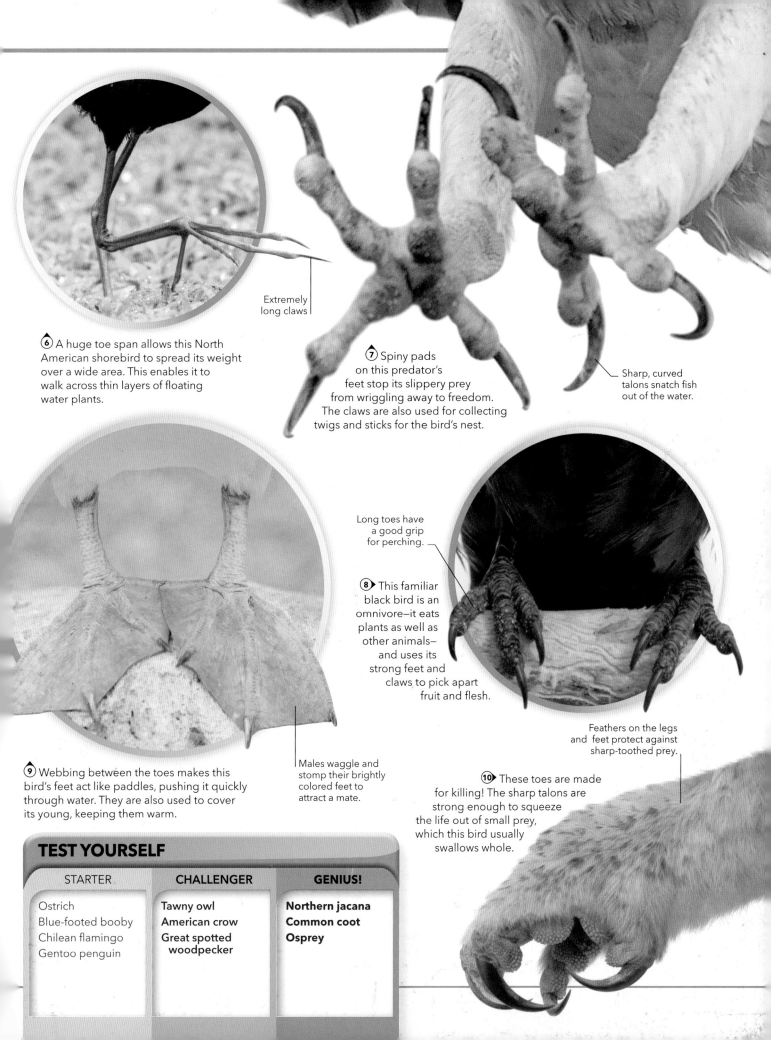

Extremely
long claws

⑥ A huge toe span allows this North American shorebird to spread its weight over a wide area. This enables it to walk across thin layers of floating water plants.

⑦ Spiny pads on this predator's feet stop its slippery prey from wriggling away to freedom. The claws are also used for collecting twigs and sticks for the bird's nest.

Sharp, curved talons snatch fish out of the water.

Long toes have a good grip for perching.

⑧▶ This familiar black bird is an omnivore—it eats plants as well as other animals—and uses its strong feet and claws to pick apart fruit and flesh.

⑨ Webbing between the toes makes this bird's feet act like paddles, pushing it quickly through water. They are also used to cover its young, keeping them warm.

Males waggle and stomp their brightly colored feet to attract a mate.

Feathers on the legs and feet protect against sharp-toothed prey.

⑩▶ These toes are made for killing! The sharp talons are strong enough to squeeze the life out of small prey, which this bird usually swallows whole.

TEST YOURSELF

STARTER	CHALLENGER	GENIUS!
Ostrich	**Tawny owl**	**Northern jacana**
Blue-footed booby	**American crow**	**Common coot**
Chilean flamingo	**Great spotted woodpecker**	**Osprey**
Gentoo penguin		

1 Wading through shallow saline (salty) marshes, this black-capped bird hunts small animals by sweeping its super-sensitive bill from side to side in the water.

Long, upturned bill

Adults grow up to 4 ft (1.2 m) tall.

2 This bird uses its strong, orange beak to prise open shellfish. It makes a very basic nest by simply scraping out a patch in the ground along the shore, often among pebbles.

3 A slender, curved bill enables this North American bird to probe deep into soft mud, looking for insects and shellfish. Its flight song is made up of trills and whistles.

4 This noisy, aggressive bird is so common in coastal towns that it has become known as a pest. Named for a type of fish, it has black wingtips.

Its hooked bill has a distinctive red patch.

5 With wings that work like flippers, this expert swimmer feeds on small fish in the icy waters around Antarctica. It breeds in huge colonies on the Antarctic ice.

Coastal birds

Coastlines around the world, including those in the frozen Arctic and Antarctic regions, are home to many birds. Some stay close to land, feeding along muddy or sandy shores. Others spend most of their lives fishing far out at sea, and only visit land once a year to lay eggs and care for their young. Many of these birds nest together to breed in vast, noisy cliffside colonies.

Jet black wing tips

Yellow-tinged plumage on the head and neck

6 This seabird is known for plunge-diving (diving swiftly from the air into the water) at speeds of up to 53 mph (86 km/h). Once under water, it hunts fish using its sharp, daggerlike bill.

Long, narrow wings help it glide on ocean breezes, conserving energy for a long flight.

(8) This bird was named for a type of ship because of the way it often soars above the waves for days at a time. It attacks other seabirds to make them cough up fish they have caught—and then consumes the fish.

Males inflate their red throat pouch to attract a mate.

(7) This seabird flies more than 59,650 miles (96,000 km) every year from the Arctic Circle to Antarctica and back, making the longest migration among all birds.

(9) This master soarer has a wingspan of up to 11 ft (3.5 m)—the largest of all birds. It flies low over the icy Antarctic Ocean to snatch small fish, squid, and krill from just below the surface.

(10) Also known as the "clown of the sea" for its comic waddle, this bird uses its muscular wings to dive deep into the water for food. Its colorful bill can hold more than ten small fish at once!

Black cap and crest

(11) This clever bird tries to tempt predators away from its nest by pretending to have a broken wing. It is also known as a peewit after the sound of its call.

Long, webbed toes

Spiky crest of yellow and black feathers

Red throat

(12) Rarely seen on land, this European bird can stay under water for more than a minute chasing fish. It holds its slender, sharp bill at an upturned angle while swimming and flying.

Long flight feathers

Wings must be spread out to dry, as the feathers are not waterproof.

(13) This bird jumps to move from one spot to another, rather than waddling. It lives on the shores of islands in the Antarctic Ocean and shrieks loudly to defend its territory.

(14) Found in almost all continents, this long-necked bird can dive down to 100 ft (30 m) under the surface of water in pursuit of fish.

TEST YOURSELF

STARTER
Red-throated diver
Atlantic puffin
Emperor penguin
Wandering albatross
Herring gull

CHALLENGER
Magnificent frigate bird
Arctic tern
Rockhopper penguin
Eurasian oystercatcher
Great cormorant

GENIUS!
Northern lapwing
Northern gannet
Pied avocet
Long-billed curlew

ANSWERS: 1. Pied avocet 2. Eurasian oystercatcher 3. Long-billed curlew 4. Herring gull 5. Emperor penguin 6. Northern gannet 7. Arctic tern 8. Magnificent frigate bird 9. Wandering albatross 10. Atlantic puffin 11. Northern lapwing 12. Red-throated diver 13. Rockhopper penguin 14. Great cormorant

① Waiting patiently for insects to fly past, this American bird springs into action as soon as it spots something, flying up into the air to pluck the insect from the sky.

Males have a red body and often feed the young.

Males have black plumage.

② Using its strong feet, this seed-eating bird runs up and down tree trunks and even hangs upside down from branches.

③ Common all over Europe and Asia, this bird is known for its musical song. It feeds mainly on the ground, using its beak to dig for insects and earthworms.

Its long beak is used to crack open acorns.

Males have a black mask around the beak.

Black patch around the eyes

④ Named for the plumage on its wings, this bird hunts using its hooked bill. It impales insects, small lizards, and mice on thorns to eat them later.

⑤ This large, powerful bird has a wingspan of up to 5 ft (1.5 m). It is very intelligent and eats a wide variety of food, including seeds, berries, small animals, and rotting meat.

Long flight feathers help it soar and even fly upside down at times.

Males have light-colored plumage around their face.

⑥ Using its thick, short bill to eat seeds and insects, this North American bird can be identified by its high-pitched whistling. Females are known to lay eggs in the nests of other birds.

Perching birds

More than 6,000 species of birds are known as perching birds, or passerines. These birds have toes that can grip, enabling them to perch on trees. From tiny insect-eating wrens to large, scavenging ravens, their sizes vary greatly. Some perching birds sing beautifully, and their songs help them find mates and mark their territory.

Shiny black feathers with white flecks

Males have long, decorative tail feathers, which they use in mating displays.

7 This bird hunts insects by probing the ground with its bill. When the breeding season ends, huge flocks roost together every evening, swooping through the sky like clouds of black smoke.

8 Known for mimicking the calls of many birds as well as sounds such as chainsaws, car alarms, and cameras, this Australian songbird can be up to 3¼ ft (1 m) long, including the tail.

Dark-brown upperparts

9 An excellent flier, this bird spends a lot of time in the air, hunting insects in flight. Found all over the world except Antarctica, it often builds mud nests inside buildings.

10 The bright color of this bird's plumage comes from chemicals in the seeds and berries it eats. It is mostly found in the damp woodlands of North America.

Red patch above and below the beak

Forked tail

White plumage provides camouflage in icy regions.

11 Commonly found in cities around the world, flocks of this bird are often heard before they are seen, chattering away noisily.

12 This hardy little bird breeds in the icy Arctic, building its nests farther north than any other perching bird.

Brown feathers on the back

13 Found in Australia, this songbird lives in small groups. Males have bright blue plumage on their head, cheek, and around the throat.

TEST YOURSELF

STARTER	CHALLENGER	GENIUS!
Snow bunting	**Vermilion flycatcher**	**Superb fairy-wren**
Barn swallow	**Eurasian starling**	**Superb lyrebird**
Eurasian blackbird	**Red-backed shrike**	**Northern cardinal**
House sparrow	**Brown-headed cowbird**	**Eurasian nuthatch**
Raven		

Bluish-green tail

1 The beautiful red-and-black male of this South American species has a rounded crest. It bows and jumps around to impress the brown female.

The male has a metallic green head.

2 This tiny bird's long, curved beak allows it to drink nectar from flowers. While the females are grayish brown, males have two bands of bright color around their necks.

3 Named after a precious stone, this bird from the tropical forests of Southeast Asia spends most of its time on the ground. It returns to the trees to sleep.

The crest of feathers can be fanned out.

4 Bees beware! This agile bird twists and turns as it flies, catching hundreds of bees every day. It breaks off the bee's stinger before eating it.

5 With zebra-like striped feathers, this pink bird is named for its "hoop hoop hoop" call. It nests in holes in trees, and its young can shoot their poo at predators if disturbed!

Turquoise belly

Dagger-shaped bill

Lacy fan-like crest

Pretty plumage

The feathers on a bird's body are known as its plumage. Plumage helps birds stay warm and often gives camouflage, but can also be designed to impress. The feathers can also be beautiful. In fact, birds use their dazzling colors to show off to each other and attract mates. Here are just a few of the most brilliantly feathered birds.

6 Reaching a length of 27 in (70 cm), this is one of the largest pigeons in the world. It is easily identifiable by its purple-red breast, bright blue body, and elegant crest of feathers.

ANSWERS: 1. Andean cock-of-the-rock 2. Southern double-collared sunbird 3. Emerald dove 4. European bee-eater 5. Hoopoe 6. Southern crowned pigeon 7. Resplendent quetzal 8. Racket-tailed roller 9. Ruby-throated hummingbird 10. Raggiana bird of paradise 11. Gouldian finch 12. Palawan peacock-pheasant 13. Red-crested turaco 14. Purple gallinule

7 To impress a mate, the males of this brilliantly colored tropical species swoop through the air and ripple their tails in spectacular mid-flight displays.

Short beak for eating fruit, insects, and even small frogs and lizards.

8 The distinctive, long tail feathers of this African bird have wide, flat tips, making them look a little like spoons or paddles.

9 Growing to a mere 3½ in (9 cm), this tiny bird buzzes around drinking nectar from flowers. The males have a vivid red patch on the throat.

Long, thin, straight bill to drink nectar from flowers.

A cloud of soft pink feathers surrounds the bird during display.

10 Fanning out their flamboyant maroon and golden-brown feathers, males of this species try to attract females with an elaborate bowing dance.

11 This multi-colored Australian bird has three color types, with heads that could be red, black, or yellow. It was named after a British ornithologist.

The male has green-gold, shiny tail streamers that can be up to 26 in (65 cm) long.

12 This glorious game bird lives only on one island in the Philippines. With its iridescent feathers and green crest, the male displays to females by fanning out its tail and dancing.

Bright blue "eyespots" on tail

13 Named for its bright head feathers, this beautiful bird lives only in Angola, Africa. It usually hides in the trees, where it remains motionless for hours at a time.

14 Bright yellow legs that end in long toes allow this water bird to walk across floating plants. It lives in freshwater swamps and builds floating nests for its eggs.

TEST YOURSELF

STARTER	CHALLENGER	GENIUS!
Ruby-throated hummingbird	Raggiana bird of paradise	Racket-tailed roller
Hoopoe	Palawan peacock-pheasant	Purple gallinule
European bee-eater	Southern crowned pigeon	Red-crested turaco
Emerald dove	Andean cock-of-the-rock	Resplendent quetzal
Southern double-collared sunbird		Gouldian finch

Nests and eggs

All birds lay eggs. Most of them build nests to house their eggs, and keep them warm by sitting on them until they hatch. Once hatched, some chicks are immediately capable of finding food, while others are completely helpless and need their parents to feed them and keep them warm for several weeks.

How to build a nest like a weaver

02. Weave the grass around the ring to make it sturdy. Sit on it to check that it can take your weight. Make sure it is big enough to sit in but not so large that unwelcome visitors can get in.

01. Take a long blade of fresh, bendy grass and tie it around a branch with a knot as tight as can be. Use the other end of the grass to make a ring around the branch.

Egg shapes

Bird eggs come in different shapes and sizes. Some experts think that an egg's shape is linked to how much its parents fly—birds that fly long distances have sleek bodies and so lay narrow eggs.

Oval
This is the most common shape of eggs among birds.

Near-spherical
Eggs of this shape are usually laid by birds that fly for short distances.

Conical
Birds that fly a lot tend to lay longer, more conical eggs.

Eggs

Eggs need to be kept warm for the chicks inside to develop properly.

Hatchlings

Featherless and blind, the newly hatched chicks rely on their parents for food.

Growing up

Once hatched, chicks of songbirds–such as this blue tit–need constant feeding by their parents. They only leave the nest after they have learned to fly.

Adult

Nine-day-old chicks

Feathers begin to grow, and the chicks' eyes open.

Two-week-old chicks

With plumage all over their bodies, the chicks are ready to leave the nest.

I don't believe it

The bee hummingbird builds the world's smallest nest, which is only about 1 in (2.5 cm) wide–shorter than an average paperclip!

Moving into town

White storks are often found in urban areas in central Europe. They build massive nests on top of tall buildings or lampposts.

03. Weave a roof over the ring. Let your potential mate inspect it, and if she approves, finish weaving the nest until it is strong enough to hold the eggs.

Nesting colonies

Some birds nest together in colonies to reduce the risk of an attack by predators. King penguin colonies can contain hundreds of thousands of birds.

Amazing nests

Long-tailed tits build bottle-shaped nests using spiderwebs, lichen, and feathers. As the chicks grow bigger, the nest stretches to accommodate them.

Bee-eaters use their beaks and feet to dig burrows in sandbanks. These burrows can be up to 3 ft (1 m) deep, and end in a nesting chamber.

House martins often build their nests along the edges of buildings. They layer beakfuls of wet mud on top of each other, letting the mud dry out and harden to form a nest.

7

MAMMALS

Bathing buddies

There are more than 6,000 species of mammals on the planet. Some, like these giraffes, zebras, and antelopes, live in perfect harmony. At Etosha National Park in Namibia, they are regularly seen together, drinking or bathing in a watering hole.

Types of mammals

Placentals

There are just three groups of mammals, and the majority are placental mammals. These give birth to babies that have developed inside the mother's body, nourished by an organ called a placenta.

Marsupials

The animals in this group are born before being fully developed. Until they are fully formed, they live in a pouch on the mother's body, and feed on milk.

Monotremes

Instead of giving birth to live young, platypuses and echidnas—which make up this group—lay eggs, and are all found in Australia and New Guinea.

How to parent like a monkey

01. Hold your baby tightly in your arms to keep it safe as you leap through the trees.

Mammals

Found in every habitat on Earth, mammals are vertebrates (animals with a backbone) and are warm blooded—they can generate body heat from the food they eat. They include an array of creatures, from tiny shrews to huge whales. Most mammals have hair for warmth, and nearly all bear live young that feed on their mother's milk.

02. Feed your baby regularly on milk throughout its first year.

Mammal moves

Mammals can move in many ways. Here are some of their main ways to get about.

Walk: During a drought, rhinos can walk for up to 10 miles (16 km) to find water.

Run: Among the fastest mammals, springboks can run at a speed of up to 55 mph (88 km/h).

Hop: Kangaroo rats may be small, but they can jump up to 9 ft (2.75 m) high.

Climb: Red squirrels use their sharpclaws and powerful legs to climb trees.

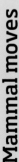

03. Kiss the baby to keep it happy, but tell it off when it is naughty. When it is old enough, teach it how to find its own food, and how to call out to its friends.

Biggest and smallest

108 ft (33 m)

6 ft (1.8 m)

1⅓ in (34 mm)

The world's largest mammal, the blue whale, lives in all oceans except the Arctic. It can weigh up to 220 tons–heavier than 25 adult elephants!

Found in caves in parts of Thailand and Myanmar, the Kitti's hog-nosed bat is the world's smallest mammal–slightly bigger than a bumblebee.

I don't believe it

Goats may not look like great climbers but some of them can scale near-vertical cliffs using their tough, clasping hooves to grip tiny crevices.

Clever creatures

Raccoons are highly intelligent, and can use their hands with great skill to open doors and locks, take the lids off jars, and break into bird feeders.

In numbers

30,000
The number of ants and termites a giant anteater can eat in a day.

22
The number of hours a koala can sleep at a stretch.

5 miles
(8 km) The distance from which a lion's roar can be heard.

Fly: Bats, such as the flying fox, can fly at a speed of up to 25 mph (40 km/h).

Glide: Flying squirrels can glide a distance of up to 492 ft (150 m).

Swing: Gibbons use their long arms to swing from branch to branch.

Swim: The paddle-like flippers of whales enable them to swim with ease.

① Gliding up to 165 ft (50 m) through the air, this nocturnal creature uses its skin flaps to help it leap from tree to tree in search of sweet sap, nectar, and insects.

The long, bushy tail is used like a rudder to guide the animal while it glides through the air.

② With distinctive stripes across its back, this carnivorous (meat-eating) marsupial finds its termite prey using its sharp sense of smell.

Its long, sticky tongue helps suck up termites.

③ Native to Australia, this creature sits for hours in eucalyptus trees, resting on its thickly padded rump, and eating as much as 2¼ lb (1 kg) of leaves a day.

Woolly fur repels rain water.

Huge ears detect moving insects, even when under the soil.

④ This rabbitlike animal is mostly found in deserts and dry areas. It can dig burrows up to 6½ ft (2 m) deep.

A thick, long tail helps maintain balance on branches.

Despite small ears, it has excellent hearing.

Thick, coarse fur

⑤ Found in the forests of New Guinea, this marsupial is known for its incredible tree-climbing skills. It can climb up to 110 ft (33 m)—higher than a 10-story building!

⑥ A bearlike appearance gives this Indonesian animal its name. It uses its claws and tail to swing between tree branches.

⑦ This stocky grass-eater has powerful claws and muscular legs, ideal for digging tunnels, where it hides by day. It can grow to a length of 3¾ ft (1.15 m).

Dark fur helps camouflage it in the treetops.

Marsupials

From sleepy leaf-eaters to powerful jumpers, marsupials—or pouched mammals—come in all shapes and sizes. They all nurture their young in a pouch or flap under the mother's skin. Here, the babies—known as joeys—are protected until they are ready to enter the world.

Its strong tail acts like an extra limb to grip branches.

8 ▶ This crafty North American creature can play dead when in danger. It lies still for hours with its eyes and mouth open, and sometimes gives off a horrible, rotten smell, too.

9 ▶ This aggressive nocturnal hunter, known for its wide gape, has one of the most powerful bites of any mammal.

Thick fur gives it protection from the sun.

10 The largest of all marsupials, this mighty mammal can grow up to 6½ ft (2 m) tall from nose to tail, and can weigh around 200 lb (90 kg).

Powerful legs allow it to leap across more than 29½ ft (9 m) when making an escape.

Its muscular tail is used as an extra leg to propel it forward.

11 Also known as a narrow-footed marsupial mouse, this small animal grows up to 4½ in (12 cm) long and has a slim tail.

TEST YOURSELF

STARTER
Common wombat
Red kangaroo
Koala
Tasmanian devil

CHALLENGER
Virginia opossum
Sugar glider
Doria's tree kangaroo
Sulawesi bear cuscus

GENIUS!
Slender-tailed dunnart
Numbat
Greater bilby

Eyes are covered with a thick layer of skin.

The scaly tail can be up to 11½ in (29 cm) long.

A sensitive snout gives it an excellent sense of smell.

1 Named for its light-colored fur, this tiny animal is only 3½ in (9 cm) long. It uses its broad claws to "swim" through the sand of the Namib Desert in Africa.

Thick fur carries algae which turns it green, providing camouflage in the trees.

3 This furry creature from Southeast Asia produces a powerful stink—similar to urine or rotten garlic—to mark its territory.

Three curved claws give it a powerful grip.

2 Living among the trees in the rainforests of Central and South America, this animal is believed to be the world's slowest-moving mammal.

Strong hind legs help it hang from tree branches.

Insect eaters and sloths

Insect eaters have developed special features for hunting their favorite food—bugs. Some have long, pointed snouts and sticky tongues, while others have sharp teeth to crunch through hard animal shells. Sloths are mostly herbivores (plant eaters), although some eat insects too. They tend to be sluggish creatures with slow digestion.

Short, bristly fur has black, brown, and white stripes.

Velvety fur

Its long snout hides a sticky tongue for lapping up its prey.

4 Named for its little tail, this creature spends most of its life underground. It uses its venomous saliva to paralyze its prey.

5 With a tongue that can flick almost three times a second, this animal can eat lots of insects very quickly. It also has a keen sense of smell.

6 ▶ A gardener's best friend, this creature will eat up all the slugs in your vegetable patch! When threatened, it curls up into a prickly ball to deter predators.

Sensitive nose has more touch sensors than a human hand.

7 ▶ With eyes so small that it can barely see, this animal uses its nose and whiskers to detect prey, such as an earthworm, then gulps it down in less than a second.

8 ▶ This animal loves to feast on ants and termites. Its muscular body allows it to tunnel into the ground very quickly to find food, dig a burrow, or escape predators.

Large front claws help it dig into termite mounds.

9 ▶ Protected by its shell of tough, bony armour, this American creature is mostly found in forests and grasslands. It hunts by night and can sleep for up to 16 hours a day.

Babies ride on their mother's back for up to one year.

Plates growing in the skin protect it from predators.

10 ▶ Found in Madagascar, this striped animal is 7½ in (19 cm) long. When threatened, it uses its sharp spikes to defend itself.

A long, pointed snout helps it find food.

The bushy tail is used as a fifth leg for balance.

TEST YOURSELF

STARTER
European hedgehog
Giant anteater
Three-toed sloth
Star-nosed mole

CHALLENGER
Northern short-tailed shrew
Grant's golden mole
Nine-banded armadillo

GENIUS!
Lowland streaked tenrec
Aardvark
Moonrat

① Found in thickly forested parts of Asia, this large mammal weighs almost 4 lb (1.8 kg) and grows up to 3¼ ft (1 m) in length. Its large eyes give it sharp night vision.

Flaps of skin between the legs help it glide.

Thick fur keeps it warm through the winter months.

② This solitary animal, also known as a "woodchuck," digs extensive burrows with multiple rooms under open meadows and farms.

③ Considered the engineer of the animal world, this clever creature can construct river dams up to 1,600 ft (500 m) long using logs that it cuts from trees using its sharp front teeth.

Sensitive whiskers allow it to find food in the dark.

Sharp claws for defense

The paddle-like tail helps it swim fast.

⑤ From South America, this mountain dweller has large, nearly hairless ears with sharp hearing. Its tail can detach when grabbed by a predator!

⑥ Found in the forests of South America, this animal has white stripes and spots on its coat. A slow mover, it feasts on fruits, shoots, and leaves.

Distinctive yellow-gray fur

④ This familiar rodent is found all over the world. Common in urban areas, it uses its sensitive whiskers to find food in the dark.

⑦ Found in the forests of Brazil and Argentina, this long-legged animal is a fast runner. It often buries seeds and forgets about them, allowing plants to grow.

The long tail is used for balance and to regulate body temperature.

TEST YOURSELF

STARTER	CHALLENGER	GENIUS!
Eurasian red squirrel	**Capybara**	**False paca**
Brown rat	**Hazel dormouse**	**Azara's agouti**
Red and white giant flying squirrel	**Groundhog**	**Common degu**
Cape porcupine	**Long-eared jerboa**	
American beaver		

ANSWERS: 1. Red and white giant flying squirrel 2. Groundhog 3. American beaver 4. Brown rat 5. Common degu 6. False paca 7. Azara's agouti 8. Capybara 9. Eurasian red squirrel 10. Hazel dormouse 11. Long-eared jerboa 12. Cape porcupine

The ears fold back to stop water from collecting inside them.

8 The largest rodent in the world, this mammal weighs up to 145½ lb (66 kg). It lives in swamps and flooded grasslands.

9 Known for its dense fur and bushy tail, this animal likes to leap across branches.

10 Only 3½ in (9 cm) long, this tiny animal lives in small family groups. It eats berries, nuts, insects, and flowers.

It has tufts on its ears, which grow longer in winter.

Toothy rodents

Large front teeth and powerful jaws make rodents expert chompers. From the tiny pygmy jerboa to the giant capybara, these furry animals come in a range of sizes. Almost half of all mammals are rodents and they thrive on all continents except Antarctica.

Ears measure 2 in (5 cm) in length.

11 Growing up to just 3¾ in (9.5 cm) this mouselike rodent has the biggest ears on Earth relative to its size, and excellent hearing.

Sharp quills up to 12 in (30 cm) long

12 When threatened, this spiky animal found in South Africa raises and rattles its sharp quills in a dramatic display, then charges backward toward the predator!

1 ▶ With distinctive black rings, this bushy tail belongs to a relative of the meerkat found in Madagascar. It is used for balance when the animal scuttles through the trees.

Thick, stiff hairs help swat flies away.

2 This giant mammal swishes its tail around when it is happy or excited. Babies hold on to the tails of adults while walking to avoid getting lost.

3 Used to swat away flies and other pesky bugs, the long, flexible tail of this striped relative of the horse swishes from side to side as the animal grazes in the open African savanna

Brushlike tuft of hair at the tip

Telling tails

Hanging, steering, swatting, swimming—mammals use their tails to do all these and more. While some move their tails around to communicate, others swish theirs to keep insects at bay, and some curl up under theirs to stay warm in cold weather. As varied in shape, size, and function as the animals they belong to, can you tell which tail is whose?

4 When this primate is looking for a mate, it covers its tail in a stinky substance and waves it in the air. The smelliest one in a group is considered the most attractive!

The flat and wide tail helps steer the animal while swimming.

5 This water-loving animal uses its tail to store half of its body fat for times when food may be scarce. Females use theirs to keep eggs warm till they hatch.

6 The tail of this creature is covered with bony plates like the rest of its body. When in danger, it rolls up into a ball, tucking its tail alongside its head to protect itself.

The long, distinctly patterned tail is also used to warn other animals of danger.

The tail can be slapped on the surface of the water to communicate.

7 This sea mammal uses its tail—which is made up of two large flaps called "flukes"— to propel its body through the water.

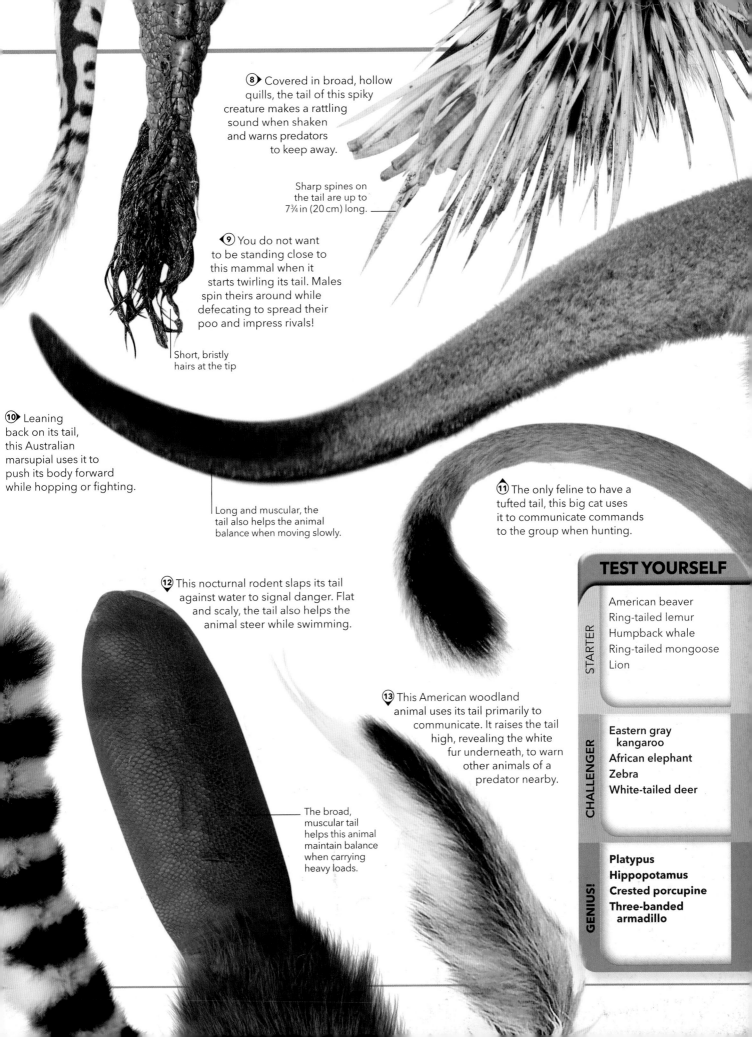

8 Covered in broad, hollow quills, the tail of this spiky creature makes a rattling sound when shaken and warns predators to keep away.

Sharp spines on the tail are up to 7¾ in (20 cm) long.

9 You do not want to be standing close to this mammal when it starts twirling its tail. Males spin theirs around while defecating to spread their poo and impress rivals!

Short, bristly hairs at the tip

10 Leaning back on its tail, this Australian marsupial uses it to push its body forward while hopping or fighting.

Long and muscular, the tail also helps the animal balance when moving slowly.

11 The only feline to have a tufted tail, this big cat uses it to communicate commands to the group when hunting.

12 This nocturnal rodent slaps its tail against water to signal danger. Flat and scaly, the tail also helps the animal steer while swimming.

13 This American woodland animal uses its tail primarily to communicate. It raises the tail high, revealing the white fur underneath, to warn other animals of a predator nearby.

The broad, muscular tail helps this animal maintain balance when carrying heavy loads.

TEST YOURSELF

STARTER
American beaver
Ring-tailed lemur
Humpback whale
Ring-tailed mongoose
Lion

CHALLENGER
Eastern gray kangaroo
African elephant
Zebra
White-tailed deer

GENIUS!
Platypus
Hippopotamus
Crested porcupine
Three-banded armadillo

Monkey business

Clever, comic, and sometimes cunning, monkeys are the pranksters of the animal world. With their long limbs and nimble fingers, these playful primates love to wrestle, steal food, and scamper across trees.

1) Mostly found living near water in the forests of Borneo, this animal is a great swimmer and survives mainly on fruits and leaves.

Males have large, drooping noses that can measure up to 3 in (7.6 cm).

Large eyes help it see clearly at night.

2) This nocturnal creature uses its long legs to leap between trees. It is one of the few species of monkey that forage for food at night.

3) A flattened nose and beautiful fur give this primate its name. It lives in high forests in China, and needs a thick coat to protect it from the cold.

White fur on the face and chest

4) Found all over Africa, this large animal has a greenish-gray coat, for which it is named. Hairless pads on its bottom help it sit on trees without falling off.

5) This round-headed primate from the tropical forests of South America is thought to be the smartest of all monkeys. It is always active and eats plants, fruits, and small animals.

Its shiny coat changes color with the seasons.

Crest runs from the forehead to the crown.

6) This shy Indian primate is among the most endangered of its kind. It spends most of its time high in the forest canopy.

7) Living on the Indonesian island of Sulawesi, this animal is covered in black fur except on its pink bottom.

The animal grows a white beard when it is six weeks old.

8 Named after a French-Italian explorer and around 21¼ in (54 cm) long (not including its tail), this animal is found in swampy African forests. When in danger it sits perfectly still for hours, until the threat has passed.

The long tail is used for balance when climbing trees.

10 Easily identified by its magnificent white mustache, this tiny monkey is about the same size as a gray squirrel.

9 Named for the color of the fur on its back, this primate is found in the Virunga Mountains of Africa. It eats bamboo and also lives on bamboo trees.

Dense yellow bristles on its cheeks and forehead

ark brown crest on the head

11 Also known as a spectacled leaf monkey because it looks like it is wearing glasses, this animal is born with bright orange fur which turns gray in adulthood.

Its flat nose prevents frostbite.

Long fingers allow it to grasp branches easily.

12 Weighing just 3½ oz (100 g), this is the smallest monkey in the world. It runs up and down trees, making holes in the bark and then lapping up the sap.

The tail can be longer than its body.

Males have a red, bald patch on the chest.

13 Eating mainly grass, this mountain dweller uses its nimble fingers to pick blades of grass and herbs. Adult males have long front teeth, which they bare to warn off rivals.

TEST YOURSELF

STARTER

White-faced capuchin
Pygmy marmoset
Golden snub-nosed monkey
Northern night monkey

CHALLENGER

Proboscis monkey
Gelada
Emperor tamarin
Golden monkey
Olive baboon

GENIUS!

De Brazza's monkey
Gee's golden langur
Dusky leaf monkey
Celebes crested macaque

Long, strong arms

1 Also known as the white-handed gibbon, this Southeast Asian primate lives high up in the trees and feeds on fruit. A ring of white hair surrounds its black face.

2 With deep, booming calls that can be heard up to 2 miles (3.25 km) away, this Asian animal is the largest in the gibbon family. It can grow up to 36 in (90 cm) tall.

The throat sac is inflated to amplify its call.

3 Native to the Indonesian island of Java, this animal is known for its fluffy gray fur and dark cap. Males make a hooting noise to defend their territory.

Babies cling to their mothers when climbing.

4 At more than 440 lb (200 kg)—roughly the weight of two and a half adult humans—this African primate is the largest of all apes. Males defend the family group by beating on their chest to scare rivals away.

A ridge on the skull anchors powerful jaw muscles.

Bare skin on its face darkens with age.

5 This clever creature found in African rainforests uses tools to find food—it has been known to sharpen sticks to spear bush babies hiding in tree holes.

It uses its knuckles to walk on all fours.

Ape antics

The closest living relatives of human beings, apes are highly intelligent. This group of animals consists of great apes, such as gorillas, orangutans, and chimpanzees, and lesser apes, or gibbons, which are usually smaller. All apes have opposable thumbs (they can pinch their thumb and fingers together), which allows them to pick up and hold objects.

Domed forehead with brown fur

Arms can be twice as long as its body.

6 Almost entirely vegetarian, this great ape is found in the swamps and lowland forests of Central Africa. Its jaw muscles and teeth are adapted for chewing plants.

Long fingers help it hang from branches.

7 This critically endangered Asian primate can swing between trees at speeds of up to 35 mph (56 km/h). Named for its crest, it has a golden or black coat.

8 Spending most of its life high up in the canopy, this Southeast Asian animal builds two nests every day by bending branches— a day nest and a night nest. It can have an arm span of up to 7½ ft (2.25 m)!

Both feet and hands are able to grip branches.

Dominant males have fleshy cheek pads.

9 Living in trees as well as on the ground in groups led by females, this great ape is found in the tropical rainforests of Central Africa. It eats fruit, eggs, and insects.

10 This red-haired Asian primate lives primarily in trees, where it feeds on bark, fruit, and insects. Adult males have a prominent mustache and beard.

Woolly fur keeps it warm high in the treetops.

① Native to the savanna and dry forests south of the Sahara Desert in Africa, this big-eyed creature is an excellent climber. It can leap up to 25 times its body length from branch to branch.

Rounded fingers and toes for clinging to branches

② Also known as "softly-softly" for the way it moves without making any noise, this African animal has pincerlike hands that help it climb trees slowly and steadily.

③ This animal has eyes bigger than its brain—the biggest eyes of any mammal, relative to its size. In fact the eyes are so large they do not rotate in their sockets, but its head can turn almost a full circle.

Tree dwellers

Eating, sleeping, playing, and even raising their young high up in the canopy, lemurs, bushbabies, and their relatives are arboreal—or tree-living—primates. They have long fingers and toes that give them a firm grip on branches. Most only come out under the cover of darkness, but a few love to bask in the sun.

④ While fruit makes up most of this animal's diet, it also uses its long snout to feed on pollen and nectar inside flowers.

Rust-colored fur blends into dried leaves when it is on the ground.

Its raised tail acts as a signal to keep the group together.

⑤ Living in groups known as troops, this primate from Madagascar is known for its long, black-and-white striped tail.

6 Like bees, this animal is good at spreading pollen, which sticks to the fur around its face and gets transported from tree to tree. It uses its deft fingers to open flowers and eat the nectar inside.

Adult males are around 8½ in (22 cm) long.

White, furry stripes on face

Black, gray, and white patches of fur help camouflage it among the trees.

7 This Asian animal and its close relatives are the world's only venomous primates. It makes an oil in its elbow that is venomous when mixed with spit, then licks this over its babies to protect them.

Large, batlike ears can be folded down when leaping through thorny bushes.

8 The largest lemur, growing up to 28 in (70 cm) in length, this animal is the only one of its family that communicates through song.

White ruff of fur around its face

Males have longer ears than females.

9 About 2½ in (6.3 cm) long, this is the smallest of the primates. It weighs just 1 oz (30 g)—about the same as a AA battery!

10 Found in southern Africa, this creature lives in pairs or small groups. Flexible and agile, it is an expert hunter and can snatch insects from the air.

Large feet for gripping very thick branches

TEST YOURSELF

STARTER	CHALLENGER	GENIUS!
Ring-tailed lemur	**Pygmy mouse lemur**	**Senegal bush baby**
Black-and-white ruffed lemur	**Javan slow loris**	**Southern lesser galago**
Red-ruffed lemur	**Philippine tarsier**	**Potto**
		Indri

Short fur traps air and repels water to keep the animal warm.

1 This flippered animal has two layers of hair—a coarse outer coat, and a soft inner pelt. The outer hairs protect the inner fur and skin from extreme cold.

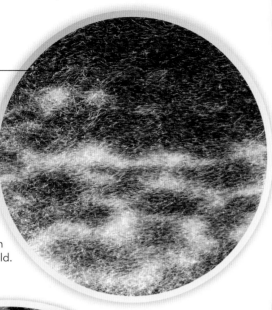

2 This animal has a pattern of black and white stripes that confuses predators when seen in a herd full of striped bodies.

3 Green algae grows on the surface of this slow-moving animal's fur, which is also home to moths and other insects.

4 The rosettes on the fur of this big cat help it hide in dense foliage when stalking its prey.

5 Thick fur keeps this bushy-tailed rodent warm in winter. In summer, it sheds its thick coat to keep cooler under the warm sun.

6 Short, velvety gray fur helps this small animal move easily through soil while digging burrows. It spends most of its life underground.

7 A coat of short, coarse hair keeps this Australian mammal warm, while its long spines protect it from predators.

TEST YOURSELF

STARTER	CHALLENGER	GENIUS!
Northern giraffe	**Leopard**	**Lesser hedgehog tenrec**
Zebra	**Red squirrel**	**Common seal**
Cheetah	**European mole**	**Sea otter**
Black panther	**Sloth**	**Tapir**
	Short-beaked echidna	

Classy coats

All mammals are covered in a coat of hair—wool, fur, or spines—made of a substance called keratin. This coat helps them control their body temperature and survive in different environments. Patterns such as stripes, spots, or blotches also help them hide or blend into their surroundings.

8▶ This shy baby animal's patterned fur helps it hide in the dappled light of the rainforest floor as it searches for food with its trunklike nose.

Pattern of white markings on light brown fur is unique to each individual.

9 This tall land animal has short, dense fur, which protects its body from the dry heat of sub-Saharan Africa.

◀10 This sprinter's black, furry spots grow out of the darker patches on its skin underneath.

11 The silky fur of this big cat found in Asia and Africa gets its color from a large amount of melanin—a dark pigment. The faint spots or rosettes on the coat are visible in sunlight.

There are around 950,000 hairs in every square inch of fur.

12 Unlike other marine animals, this creature does not have a layer of fat to keep it warm. Its dense water-resistant fur does the job instead.

13 Named after another spiky mammal, this small creature curls up into a ball when it feels threatened. This makes its sharp spines stick out, keeping predators away.

Night senses

Night vision
Big eyes allow animals to see superbly at night, and spot unsuspecting prey. The relatively small tarsier has eyes around ½ in (1.5 cm) in diameter—about the same size as its brain!

Specialized hearing
Large, sensitive ears are able to detect sounds over long distances, or the slightest movements in the dark. Bat-eared foxes can even hear tiny termites scuttling underground!

Super scent
Long snouts allow animals, such as brown bears, to hunt for food at night. A brown bear's sense of smell is 2,000 times better than a human's.

Whiskers
Big cats, such as lions, can feel things in the dark using their whiskers. The hair follicles of each whisker are packed with sensory cells that can detect the smallest movements.

Night life

As the sun goes down and you prepare yourself for a long night's sleep, some animals are just getting ready to start their day. These creatures of the night have special features for hunting, and escaping predators, in the dark. From huge eyes to funnel-like ears, these mammals have what it takes to survive and thrive at night.

I don't believe it!

Binturongs are primarily nocturnal animals and are related to mongooses. They leave a scent trail of urine, which smells like hot popcorn.

How to hunt like a lioness

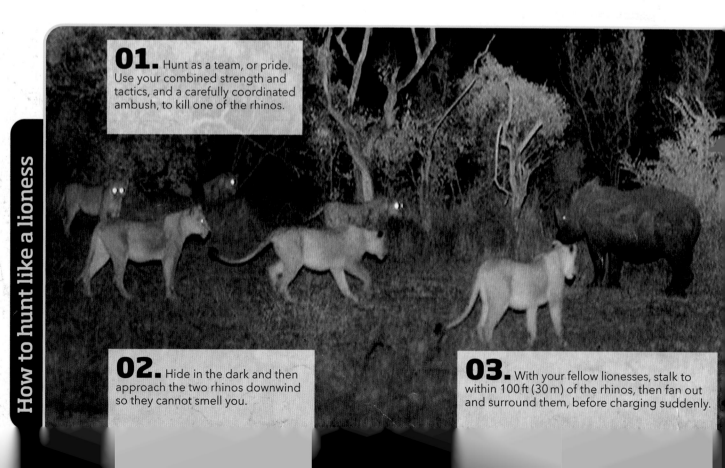

01. Hunt as a team, or pride. Use your combined strength and tactics, and a carefully coordinated ambush, to kill one of the rhinos.

02. Hide in the dark and then approach the two rhinos downwind so they cannot smell you.

03. With your fellow lionesses, stalk to within 100 ft (30 m) of the rhinos, then fan out and surround them, before charging suddenly.

15
The number of echolocation calls per second made by a hunting bat.

200
The number of earthworms a badger can consume in a single evening.

13 ft
(4 m) The distance a Spix's night monkey can leap in the dark!

Foraging for food

The aye-aye lives in Madagascar and is the world's largest nocturnal primate. It spends 80 percent of the night foraging for food. It uses its long middle finger to tap on trees, then listens to the echoes that return to detect wood-boring insects inside. Using the same finger, it then digs out the insects from beneath the bark.

Echolocation

The call of a bat is so high-pitched that humans cannot hear it. But a bat's ears are tuned in to the echoes that bounce off obstacles–such as flying insects– allowing the bat to detect and hunt prey in the dark. This ability is called echolocation.

The returning echo reaches the bat, giving it a precise location of the moth.

Sound waves bounce off the moth.

A loud clicking sound emitted by the bat moves outward.

Electric sixth sense
When hunting in murky waters, the mostly nocturnal platypus uses its bill to detect electric signals from its prey, such as fish and shrimp.

04. Target the smaller and weaker rhino. Work as a team and use your strong, sharp claws to attack by clinging to the rhino and dragging it down.

05. Use your massive, stabbing canine teeth and cheek teeth with bladelike edges to slice through the tough hide of the rhino.

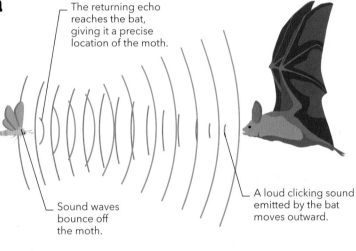

06. Chances of killing a huge, powerful rhino are slim, but if you are lucky, you will kill one of them and eat well.

Aardvarks spend their nights digging burrows to look for food. They can dig 2 ft (0.6 m) in 15 seconds.

The call of the lesser bulldog bat is 137 decibels–louder than the jet engine of a passenger aircraft.

Weighing just 0.06 oz (1.8 g), Etruscan shrews are one of the smallest nocturnal mammals. They prey on insects, worms, snails, and spiders.

Canine crew

Known for more than just their bark and bite, these predatory canines are intelligent, social animals with a sharp sense of smell. Some of them can withstand extreme temperatures, from hot deserts to freezing Arctic regions. Others may be seen roaming city streets in the dead of the night.

(1) Found in North America, Europe, Asia, and Northern Africa, this furry animal has adapted to life in all kinds of habitats, including farmland and busy cities.

Thick fur keeps this animal warm in winter but is shed in the summer to stop the body from overheating.

(2) This African animal hunts in packs of up to 20 individuals. It can sprint at a speed of up to 44 mph (71 km/h).

Big, round ears radiate heat to keep its body cool.

(3) Closely related to foxes, this Asian masked mammal has thick fur that changes color with the seasons, and short, rounded ears.

(4) This midsize wild dog is found only in Australia. It does not bark, but howls like a wolf.

Short, coarse fur is tawny in color.

White patches on muzzle, chest, and feet

(5) The ancestor of all domestic dogs, this animal was once hunted and endangered. Its strong, muscular legs help it run easily on uneven terrain.

7 Capable of withstanding temperatures as low as –58°F (–50°C), this hardy creature is known for its beautiful white winter coat.

Black muzzle

6 This North American animal is known for howling to lay claim to its territory or greet family members.

It wraps its bushy tail around itself for warmth like a blanket.

8 A resident of South American forests, this canine is sometimes preyed on by big cats such as jaguars and pumas. Its thick, red mane stands erect when it senses danger.

Very long legs help it see above tall grass.

9 Living in dry habitats, this short-snouted animal gets its name from its thick coat. It is a scavenger and survives on leftovers from other animals.

10 This short, stocky canine from Central and South America lives in small packs in forests and low-lying bush. It is an excellent swimmer and can even dive underwater.

Large ears help it lose heat and stay cool in the desert.

Partially webbed toes help it swim fast.

Large toes support its weight while running fast.

Bushy tail with a black tip

Pointed ears are lined with white fur

12 Also called the "whistling dog," this Asian animal can whistle, scream, mew, and cluck like a chicken.

11 The smallest of all wild canine species, this animal grows to a maximum length of 16 in (41 cm). It is found mostly in the scorching Sahara Desert in Africa.

13 Native to just one country in Africa, this species is the rarest of its kind on Earth. It hunts small mammals such as grass rats.

TEST YOURSELF

STARTER	CHALLENGER	GENIUS!
Gray wolf	**African wild dog**	**Dhole**
Red fox	**Coyote**	**Bush dog**
Arctic fox	**Raccoon dog**	**Ethiopian wolf**
Dingo	**Maned wolf**	**Fennec fox**
Golden jackal		

① One of the most colorful bat species in the world, this flying mammal from Asia can be found hanging upside down in banana trees.

② Found throughout India and parts of Southeast Asia, this species roosts in large colonies in forests and swamps. Growing up to 9 in (22 cm) in length, it is one of the largest bats in the world.

Bright orange fur warns other bats to leave it alone.

Distinctive long, furry snout

Wingspan can stretch to 5 ft (1.5 m).

Its leaf-shaped nose helps focus sound waves during echolocation.

③ This bat is found in Central and South America and is famous for feeding on the blood of animals, including birds, pigs, and horses. It uses its incredibly sharp teeth to bite these animals, and then laps up their flowing blood using its tongue.

White fur is tinted green when sunlight filters through the green leaves, hiding it from predators.

④ This bat lives in Central America and shelters under the big leaves of heliconia plants, which it shapes into tents by biting through the leaves until they collapse into an inverted V-shape. Up to 12 bats can take cover under one leaf.

Brilliant bats

The only true flying mammals, bats have adaptations, such as big ears, excellent eyesight, and an ability to find food through echolocation, that make many of them expert hunters. To hunt at night, a bat emits a high-pitched sound. When the sound waves hit an object, such as an insect, they produce an echo that helps the bat to find it.

Broad, rounded ears

⑤ This bat is one of the smallest mammals in the world and weighs just ⅕ oz (6 g). Despite its small size, it can catch and eat up to 3,000 insects in a single night.

Ears can move independently to catch the slightest movement.

⑥ Dates, apples, and apricots are the favorite foods of this flying mammal. This bat lives in caves.

The wings are also used to paddle across water.

Large ears are joined at the base.

⑦ Found in North America, the huge ears of this midsize bat make it perfectly adapted to hunting moths, flies, and beetles in the dark.

⑧ Found near bodies of water in Central and South America, this bat feeds almost exclusively on fish. Using its large feet, it can catch up to 30 fish in one night.

⑨ Snowy-white, with long ears and almost transparent wings, this Australian bat is a powerful hunter with very large teeth, and looks for prey on the ground. It eats frogs, lizards, and birds.

⑩ Found in Europe and Asia, this species has a butterfly-like fluttering flight with short glides in between. It hibernates in winter in caves, mines, and tunnels.

Males have bright orange fur.

Bare, folded skin forms a horseshoe-shaped nose leaf.

TEST YOURSELF

STARTER	CHALLENGER	GENIUS!
Honduran white bat	**Painted bat**	**Greater bulldog bat**
Townsend's big-eared bat	**Greater horseshoe bat**	**Common pipistrelle**
Ghost bat	**Indian flying fox**	**Common vampire bat**
Egyptian fruit bat		

1 White fur helps camouflage the world's biggest bear in the snow and ice. Together with a thick layer of body fat, it also enables the bear to survive the freezing Arctic winters.

A cub stays with the mother for up to 30 months.

White patch on chest

2 With strong legs and long claws, this bear is a good climber and perfectly adapted to life in the trees. It is found in the Himalayan mountains and other parts of Asia. It mostly hunts and feeds at night.

3 Found only in China, this endangered bear spends 16 hours each day eating up to 84 lb (38 kg) of bamboo shoots, its main food.

Bear facts

Legendary for their size and strength, bears use their brains and brawn to survive in the wild. These heavily built creatures have large heads, short tails, and strong limbs, which can often kill with a single, powerful blow.

Strong jaw and cheek muscles help it to crunch on the tough bamboo.

Distinctive pale circles around its eyes and snout.

Black and white fur gives good camouflage among the shadowy forest trees.

4 Living in forests in the Andes mountains in South America, this bear is mostly vegetarian. It spends much of its time in trees, where it builds a platform of sticks to sleep on and forage from.

ANSWERS: 1. Polar bear 2. Asiatic black bear 3. Giant panda 4. Spectacled bear 5. American black bear 6. Grizzly bear 7. Kodiak bear 8. Sloth bear 9. Sun bear

5 Only found in North America, this bear is incredibly strong and can flip a 308-lb (140-kg) boulder with a single paw. It is an excellent climber and will scramble up a tree when scared.

Fur has pale silvery or golden tips.

Dark, black-colored fur

6 This powerful bear measures up to 10 ft (3 m) when standing upright. It eats all summer, doubling its weight. Then, over winter when food is scarce, it spends up to six months asleep in a den.

Baby bears stay close to their mother until they are two years old.

7 Native to Alaska, this is the biggest brown bear in the world. It mainly hunts salmon, but also eats berries, grass, and occasionally elk.

It grows up to 10½ ft (3.25 m) tall and weighs as much as 1,500 lb (680 kg).

8 This bear lives in the forests of India. Using its protruding lips to suck up ants and termites, it makes slurping sounds that can be heard up to 330 ft (100 m) away.

9 Weighing just 150 lb (68 kg), this bear is the smallest in the world. It lives in the rainforests of Southeast Asia and uses its 9¾-in (25-cm) long tongue to extract honey from bees' nests.

3-in- (8-cm-) long claws are used for digging and tearing open ant nests.

In the hot tropics, its thin fur keeps it cool.

TEST YOURSELF

STARTER	CHALLENGER	GENIUS!
Giant panda	Sloth bear	Sun bear
Polar bear	American black bear	Spectacled bear
Grizzly bear	Asiatic black bear	Kodiak bear

Bird flies off just in time.

① Large paws with sharp claws give this Asian cat the grip it needs to climb trees skillfully, and even hang upside down from branches! It takes its name from the light gray rosettes on its fur.

The long tail is used for balance when climbing.

② A lone hunter, this cat from the Americas is an excellent climber. It is a night hunter and its prey includes deer and coyotes. Its many names include puma and mountain lion.

Stripes on the fur are unique to each individual.

③ This North American feline is named after its tail. It thrives in dense forests, where it stalks and hunts small prey at night, including rabbits, squirrels, and mice.

Powerful hind legs allow it to jump up to 20 ft (6 m) high.

Short, stumpy tail

The furry tail can be up to 3 ft (1 m) in length.

④ This is the biggest cat in the world and can weigh up to 660 lb (300 kg)— almost as much as fou grown men. A dense coat keeps it warm in the long, cold winters of northern Asia.

Black-tipped tufts on ears

⑤ A native of Southwest Europe, this endangered small cat has a distinctive beard. It lives in open scrubland and feeds on rabbits, ducks, and partridges.

Wild cats

This group of meat-eating, furry mammals includes big and small wild cats. Sharp teeth and claws, keen senses, and amazing agility make them ferociously effective predators. Interestingly, small wild cats only purr while most big cats can roar.

ANSWERS: 1. Clouded leopard 2. Cougar 3. Bobcat 4. Siberian tiger 5. Iberian lynx 6. Fishing cat 7. Serval 8. Cheetah 9. European wildcat 10. African lion

⑥ This stocky cat loves the water. Its partially webbed feet help it swim and walk around muddy wetlands in South and Southeast Asia.

⑦ Big ears give this African cat such sharp hearing that it can detect rodents scuttling under the ground. The spots and stripes on its light-colored coat give good camouflage on grassy plains.

Long legs help it hunt small prey in tall grass.

Powerful hind legs help propel it forward to run faster.

⑧ The world's fastest mammal, this cat can accelerate from 0 to 58 mph (93 km/h) in just 3 seconds! Its slender build and muscular tail help it to veer left and right while sprinting at high speeds after its most agile prey, gazelles.

⑨ This may look very similar to a domestic tabby cat but it is a ferocious predator, hunting smaller mammals such as hares, mice, and voles.

⑩ The only big cat known to live in family groups, called prides, this feline feeds on hoofed mammals. The prides are defended by the males, easily recognizable by their majestic manes, but the females are the primary hunters.

Its bushy, ringed tail has a blunt, black tip.

TEST YOURSELF

STARTER
African lion
Siberian tiger
Cheetah
Cougar

CHALLENGER
Iberian lynx
Fishing cat
Bobcat

GENIUS!
Clouded leopard
Serval
European wildcat

Distinctive black and white stripes on the face

1 This endangered mammal moves into the burrows of prairie dogs and preys on them. It is identifiable by the masklike patches that frame its eyes, and its black feet.

2 The strong front paws of this European animal are perfect for digging huge burrows known as setts.

White underside

3 Measuring just 10 in (26 cm) in length, this creature might be small, but it is also ferocious. It can eat more than half of its body weight in one day.

Furry hunters

Despite their harmless appearance, mustelids (members of the weasel family) are formidable predators who can take down prey more than twice their size. Most mustelids are carnivores. They are distant relatives of raccoons and skunks who are omnivores—they will eat anything!

4 Living in the tropical forests of Central and South America, this tree dweller has a light brown pattern on its chest, which is unique to each individual.

Brownish-gray body

The tail helps spread its musk, a substance with a strong smell, to mark its territory.

6 This animal has a long body and a pointy head with a white stripe that runs across its forehead. It eats a range of food including fruit, worms, and small animals.

Large, strong claws for climbing

Flipper-like feet for swimming

5 Found in almost all African countries south of the Sahara Desert, this freshwater mammal is quick at catching its favorite foods—frogs, worms, fish, and crabs.

ANSWERS: 1. Black-footed ferret 2. European badger 3. Least weasel 4. Tayra 5. African clawless otter 6. Greater grison 7. Striped skunk 8. Honey badger 9. Wolverine 10. European pine marten 11. Stoat 12. Sea otter 13. Raccoon

7 This striped carnivore can spray a foul-smelling substance from the rear end of its body at predators more than 10 ft (3 m) away.

The tail is raised as a sign of warning.

Its thick skin can withstand bee stings.

Broad feet stop it from sinking in the snow.

8 With sharp claws and strong jaws to tear through frozen meat, this solitary hunter can take down prey as large as reindeer. It can grow up to 5 ft (1.5 m) in length.

Its white winter coat helps it hide in the snow.

9 Described as the world's most fearless animal, this mustelid likes to pick a fight. Its bite is strong enough to crack a tortoise shell!

10 Found in wooded areas throughout Europe, this animal is named after its preferred tree. It can jump as far as 20 ft (6 m) between trees to catch its prey.

11 Slightly larger than a weasel, this animal has been known to mesmerize prey with a dance before attacking it.

12 This skillful swimmer often sleeps on its back, floating on water. It uses rocks to crack open sea urchins and slurps out the insides.

Air trapped in its thick fur helps it float easily on its back.

The long, bushy tail helps it balance when leaping.

13 Looking like a masked bandit, many of these North American mammals have moved from the country into cities, where they are often found rummaging through trash cans.

TEST YOURSELF

STARTER

Least weasel
Sea otter
European badger
Raccoon
Striped skunk

CHALLENGER

Wolverine
Honey badger
Black-footed ferret
African clawless otter

GENIUS!

Stoat
Greater grison
Tayra
European pine marten

Bite size

The teeth and jaws of animals vary greatly in size and shape, depending on their diet. Carnivores (meat eaters) usually have large, pointed canines that help them rip flesh from bones, while herbivores (plant eaters) need flatter teeth to squash and grind plant matter. Omnivores eat both plants and meat, and so need both kinds of teeth.

① To eat, this expert swimmer sucks seawater containing krill into its mouth. When it pushes the water back out, its interlocking teeth trap the krill inside for it to eat.

Short, flat front teeth are used to pull up plants.

② This huge, furry North American animal has no natural enemies except humans, and does not need to use its powerful bite for defense. It uses its teeth to catch fish, and to eat a variety of plants and fruit.

The canines of an adult can be up to 4 in (10 cm) long.

③ Zebras, antelopes, and wildebeest are food for this big cat. It uses its powerful canines to tear meat apart, and its sharp back teeth to break it down.

④ With fewer teeth than other mammals, this animal uses its tongue to latch on to grass, before biting it off with its teeth. It then chews the grass using its back teeth, in a side-to-side motion.

Front teeth are only present on the lower jaw.

⑤ This flying mammal needs razor sharp teeth to crunch through the shells of beetles, moths, and other insects.

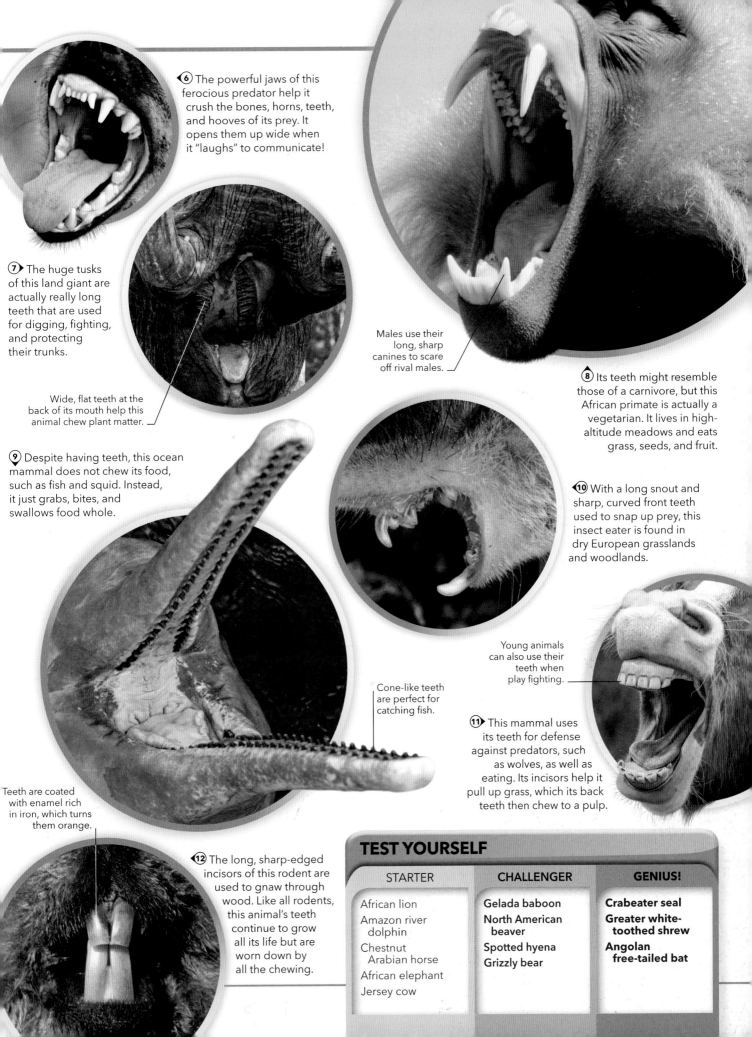

6 The powerful jaws of this ferocious predator help it crush the bones, horns, teeth, and hooves of its prey. It opens them up wide when it "laughs" to communicate!

7 The huge tusks of this land giant are actually really long teeth that are used for digging, fighting, and protecting their trunks.

Wide, flat teeth at the back of its mouth help this animal chew plant matter.

Males use their long, sharp canines to scare off rival males.

8 Its teeth might resemble those of a carnivore, but this African primate is actually a vegetarian. It lives in high-altitude meadows and eats grass, seeds, and fruit.

9 Despite having teeth, this ocean mammal does not chew its food, such as fish and squid. Instead, it just grabs, bites, and swallows food whole.

10 With a long snout and sharp, curved front teeth used to snap up prey, this insect eater is found in dry European grasslands and woodlands.

Cone-like teeth are perfect for catching fish.

Young animals can also use their teeth when play fighting.

11 This mammal uses its teeth for defense against predators, such as wolves, as well as eating. Its incisors help it pull up grass, which its back teeth then chew to a pulp.

Teeth are coated with enamel rich in iron, which turns them orange.

12 The long, sharp-edged incisors of this rodent are used to gnaw through wood. Like all rodents, this animal's teeth continue to grow all its life but are worn down by all the chewing.

TEST YOURSELF

STARTER	CHALLENGER	GENIUS!
African lion	**Gelada baboon**	**Crabeater seal**
Amazon river dolphin	**North American beaver**	**Greater white-toothed shrew**
Chestnut Arabian horse	**Spotted hyena**	**Angolan free-tailed bat**
African elephant	**Grizzly bear**	
Jersey cow		

① This horse gets its name from the Teke people of Turkmenistan in Asia. Not only is it able to cope with the extreme heat and cold of Central Asia, it also has amazing stamina and lightning-fast speed.

Short mane

Large, almond-shaped eyes

Distinctive white muzzle

Horsing around

The horse family includes more than just horses—zebras and asses are a part of it, too. All of them are highly social animals who, in the wild, live together in herds. With extremely well-developed senses and the ability to run at speed, horses come in a variety of shapes and sizes.

② This horse from Mongolia is thought to be the last truly wild species. It likes to stand head-to-tail with a mate, both flicking their tails to shoo away pests from each other's faces.

③ Native to Southern France, this horse is born with a brown or black coat, which turns gray at the age of four. In the wild, they live in herds in coastal marshes.

④ Originally from a Northern European country, this clever and spirited horse is famous for its *tölt*—a type of fast walk that is typical of this animal.

Double coat is for warmth in cold, icy weather.

⑤ This mammal's stripes are as unique as human fingerprints and, according to some scientists, could help protect the animal by confusing predators. It lives in large herds, eating grass, leaves, and fruit.

Wide, white strip called a blaze down the muzzle

Large ears help it stay cool in the hot weather.

⑥ Living in the deserts of Somalia in Africa, this animal can survive with little food and water, mostly eating bark, grass, and leaves.

Stripes on legs

Feathery hairs on lower legs

Long, thick mane protects against cold weather.

⑦ One of the most powerful horses in the world, this animal can measure up to 7 ft (2.19 m) in height. For hundreds of years it was used to pull carts on the roads and for plowing fields.

⑧ At just 42 in (107 cm) in height this horse from Scotland may be tiny compared to other horse breeds, but it is tough and can pull more than twice its own body weight.

⑨ A long, shaggy coat and large fuzzy ears make this animal easy to recognize. This species is from France.

TEST YOURSELF

STARTER
Plains zebra
Shetland pony
Shire horse

CHALLENGER
Przewalski's horse
Icelandic horse
African wild ass

GENIUS!
Poitou donkey
Camargue
Akhal-Teke

ANSWERS: 1. Akhal-Teke 2. Przewalski's horse 3. Camargue 4. Icelandic horse 5. Plains zebra 6. African wild ass 7. Shire horse 8. Shetland pony 9. Poitou donkey

Who left that?

Droppings, dung, feces, scat—poo has many names. Despite being called waste, it is actually one of the most useful substances on Earth. Animals use their poo to mark their territory, build shields for defense, and even attract mates! From large blobs and cubes to tiny pellets, poo comes in all shapes and sizes.

(1) This ferocious creature's poo is white in color because the animal eats a lot of bones, chomping through animal carcasses using its powerful jaws.

(2) Resembling small coconuts, this animal's poo reveals its diet—bark, twigs, and leaves. The furry creature also uses these materials to build dams.

The droppings contain chips of wood and sawdust.

The droppings smell of eucalyptus.

(3) The tree dweller that produces these olive-size pellets can produce up to 360 in a day, even while it is sleeping!

(4) This large primate likes to pick out and eat the seeds in its feces, which are full of undigested plant fiber from its vegetarian diet.

(5) Sausage-shaped and dark because of all the worms it eats, this burrowing mammal's poo is found in small pits called latrines. It can also contain seeds and berries.

The shape of the poo is similar to that of a human.

(6) Filled with fish bones, scales, and crayfish remains, this expert swimmer's droppings are known as spraints and are mostly found on rocks or logs near water.

TEST YOURSELF

STARTER	CHALLENGER	GENIUS!
Elephant	European badger	European beaver
Siberian tiger	Koala	Eurasian otter
European rabbit	Spotted hyena	Giant panda
Indian rhinoceros	Mountain gorilla	Wombat
	Red fox	European pine marten

ANSWERS: 1. Spotted hyena 2. European beaver 3. Koala 4. Mountain gorilla, 5. European badger 6. Eurasian otter 7. Red fox 8. Elephant 9. Indian rhinoceros 10. European pine marten 11. European rabbit 12. Giant panda 13. Siberian tiger 14. Wombat

7 This cunning creature produces fur-filled poo that has a strong, pungent smell and also contains fruit, seeds, bone fragments, and grass.

Cherry stones are often found in the droppings.

8 Because this large animal digests less than half of what it eats, its dung is full of partially digested plant matter and straw. The animal produces up to 154 lb (70 kg) of poo every day.

Large, moist blobs become hard and crumbly once dry.

10 While defecating, this expert climber likes to wriggle its hips, which results in twisted poo. Dark in color, the feces can contain berries, seeds, feathers, and bones.

The black pellets are full of grass.

9 This horned mammal stamps on and kicks apart its poo to spread its scent. Its large, rounded poo is full of fibrous plant matter.

11 The soft, pea-size droppings of this small, long-eared animal are found in clusters. It produces edible poo at night, and eats it directly out of the anus!

12 Filled with bamboo, this endangered animal's poo is yellow or green depending on whether it has been eating the stem or leaves. This creature can poo up to 40 times a day!

13 Dark and cylindrical, this big cat's poo is especially smelly because of its diet of large mammals, such as moose, buffaloes, and deer.

Undigested fur from its prey

Its shape stops it from rolling away.

14 The only animal to have poo that is shaped almost like a cube, this marsupial stacks its dung outside its home to mark its territory.

Hoofed herds

With long legs and hoofed feet, these mammals are fast runners and most live in big groups called herds. Some have horns and others have antlers, both of which come in a wide range of sizes and shapes. While antlers are mainly used to impress or fight male rivals and are shed every year, horns are a permanent feature and may be used to fend off predators.

1 This Arctic animal likes to graze on mosslike lichen—one of the few things that grow in the cold winters. Both males and females have antlers, but male antlers are larger.

2 The only animal with forked horns, which it sheds every year, this mammal has excellent eyesight. It can spot something moving up to 3 miles (5 km) away.

White neck band

Horns are widely spread out.

Dense coat for protection against extreme cold

Long, curved horns

3 With the ability to climb the steepest of mountains, this wild animal lives at heights of up to 13,123 ft (4,000 m) above sea level. Its babies are called kids.

4 This species of cattle can be identified by its all-white coat. Large males can reach a whopping 1,984 lb (900 kg)—five times heavier than the average motorcycle.

Flattened antlers

Pointed hooves for digging through snow

5 The world's largest deer, this animal from North America and Eurasia stands up to 6½ ft (2 m) tall. Unlike other deer, it usually lives a solitary life.

6 To retain water in the hot deserts of the Middle East, this animal's body is able to extract all the moisture from its poo. Its ringed horns are straight and can be up to 30 in (76 cm) in length.

White bands on ankles

The two front horns are shorter than the back two.

7 Living in the Himalayas in Asia, this heavy-set animal is built for the cold. With a double-layered hairy coat, it can tolerate temperatures as low as –40°F (–40°C).

8 This shy animal from Asia has a reddish orange coat and a tiny tail. It is easily recognized by its horns.

Russet-colored coat

9 The male of this species has impressive, branched antlers. These are used to engage in fierce battles with other males to impress the females during the breeding season.

Large ears lose heat to keep the body cool in hot weather.

10 Sprinting away at speed is easy for this animal because it has long legs in relation to its body. Living in the northern African deserts, it can go without water for a long time. Its name means "deer" in Greek.

Muscular legs for speed and agility

11 Despite its vast bulk, this North American animal can run at speeds of up to 35 mph (60 km/h). In the mating season, rival males clash their broad heads together in fierce battles.

Bristly, black hair along the bridge of its nose.

Rival males clash during the mating season.

12 Named for its dark hair, this African mammal has a tail like a horse, which it uses to swat flies. As seasons change, millions of them migrate across the plains of Africa.

TEST YOURSELF

STARTER
Red deer
White park cattle
Reindeer
Four-horned antelope

CHALLENGER
Moose
Black wildebeest
American bison
Wild goat

GENIUS!
Pronghorn
Dorcas gazelle
Domestic yak
Arabian oryx

ANSWERS: 1. Reindeer 2. Pronghorn 3. Wild goat 4. White park cattle 5. Moose 6. Arabian oryx 7. Domestic yak 8. Four-horned antelope 9. Red deer 10. Dorcas gazelle 11. American bison 12. Black wildebeest

Pig tales

Pigs love to wallow in mud to cool down because they are largely unable to sweat, and the mud protects against the sun and pests. Most of them have strong snouts to dig up food and some have curved tusks. While related, peccaries come from a different family from pigs. However, both are ungulates—hoofed mammals with an even number of toes.

1 This hog lives in African forests and builds nests that are 10 ft (3 m) wide and 3¼ ft (1 m) high to give birth in. It has sharp lower tusks that grow up to 2¾ in (7 cm) long.

2 The wild ancestor of the domestic pig, this speedy mammal can run at up to 30 mph (48 km/h). It is found in a variety of habitats in Europe, Asia, and North Africa.

3 The only species of pig in the world to migrate. Herds of up to 200 animals travel more than 310 miles (500 km) in search of food.

A male's tusks can grow to a length of about 14 in (35 cm).

Wiry whiskers grow from its jaw.

4 Weighing up to 600 lb (272 kg), this woodland creature is the world's largest wild pig. It has two large, wartlike skin growths below each eye.

5 Moving in herds of more than 100, this creature from Central and South America uses its flexible snout to sniff out fruit, nuts, and snails.

Distinctive white patch of fur around mouth and lower jaw

ANSWERS: 1. Bush pig 2. Wild boar 3. Bornean bearded pig 4. Giant forest hog 5. White-lipped peccary 6. Common warthog 7. Pygmy hog 8. Collared peccary 9. Red river hog 10. North Sulawesi babirusa

It has long bristles on its back that raise when it is threatened.

Tail is held upright when running.

6 Growths on this animal's face act as padding in fights. It has a pair of tusks on each side—a blunt upper tusk for self-defense, and a sharper lower one for digging out roots.

Sensitive snout for seeking out tasty roots

Small, almost invisible tail

7 Standing just 12 in (30 cm) tall, this hog is the smallest in the world. It is native to India and is found in pairs or family groups.

Long, pointed ears with prominent white tufts

If startled, piglets will play dead.

8 Found from the southern US to South America, this animal communicates by snorting, squealing, barking, and growling.

Pale stripe around the neck

9 This pig, which is covered in orange-red fur, loves to wallow in ponds and streams. It is a fast runner and an excellent swimmer.

Short hair on its body makes it look bald.

10 Found in the swamps and rainforests of Indonesian islands, this animal has long tusks that curve upward and can even grow back into the skull.

TEST YOURSELF

STARTER
Common warthog
Bornean bearded pig
Wild boar
Pygmy hog

CHALLENGER
Red river hog
Collared peccary
Giant forest hog

GENIUS!
Bush pig
North Sulawesi babirusa
White-lipped peccary

Two large
humps

Hair-covered horns
are used for fighting.

Thick fur protects
it from extreme
cold and heat.

② Native to Africa, this
animal feasts on the leaves of
acacia trees. It can eat up to
99 lb (45 kg) a day!

① This mammal from
the Gobi Desert in
Asia can drink up to
15 gallons (57 liters)
of water at once.

③ Found in the
mountainous areas
of South America,
this camelid spits at
attackers to defend itself.

Light brown spots
with straight,
smooth edges

The color of its coat
varies from white to
brown or black.

④ Known for
its soft and fluffy
fur, this domesticated
animal lives in herds at
altitudes higher than
13,000 ft (4,000 m).

Soft foot pads
keep it stable
on uneven
ground.

Patches
fade to white
toward feet.

Large
knees
help
support
its heavy
weight.

Hooves
and humps

Camelids—the family of mammals that includes camels, llamas,
and alpacas—and giraffes are perfectly adapted to living in
extreme climates, from scorching deserts and hot savannas
to freezing mountains. While some have large humps to store
fat, others have broad, padded hooves to stop them from
sinking into the gravel or sand.

ANSWERS: 1. Bactrian camel 2. Northern giraffe 3. Guanaco 4. Alpaca
5. Llama 6. Okapi 7. Dromedary 8. Vicuña 9. Masai giraffe

5 Standing 6 ft (1.75 m) tall, this domesticated camelid is found in the Andes Mountains. Long, banana-shaped ears give it a sharp sense of hearing.

Two rows of eyelashes keep sand out of its eyes.

Thick, oily fur keeps it dry when it rains.

White stripes on each of its legs

6 A member of the giraffe family, this shy African animal is also known as a "forest zebra." It lives in tropical rainforests and eats twigs, leaves, and fruits.

8 Only 36 in (90 cm) tall when fully grown, this South American animal is one of the smallest camelids. It is graceful and light-footed, and is well-adapted to hilly terrain.

7 This hardy creature can walk for up to 30 miles (50 km) a day. Its tough lips help it pick at hard and thorny desert plants.

Young can be up to 6½ ft (2 m) at birth!

9 The tallest animal on Earth, this mammal can reach a height of up to 18 ft (5.5 m). It only needs 5 to 30 minutes of sleep in a day.

Dark brown, leaf-shaped patches on the skin

TEST YOURSELF

STARTER
Llama
Bactrian camel
Masai giraffe

CHALLENGER
Alpaca
Dromedary
Northern giraffe

GENIUS!
Vicuña
Guanaco
Okapi

Types of marine mammals

Cetaceans
These mammals live their entire life in the ocean. They come to the surface regularly to breathe, and include whales, dolphins, and porpoises.

Pinnipeds
These fin-footed mammals include seals, sea lions, and walrusess. Pinnipeds come to land to breed or to escape predators.

Sirenians
Living primarily in tropical waters where plants grow, sirenians include the manatee and dugong. They are large, slow-moving mammals.

Fissipeds
These are mammals with separated toes. Polar bears and sea otters are considered sea mammals because they rely on the ocean for survival. They are mainly meat eaters.

How to be part of the pod

01. As you swim across the ocean, meet other bottlenose dolphins and travel in groups, or pods. Keep a lookout for superpods of up to 1,000 dolphins, and join forces with them to hunt for fish, squids, or shrimp.

02. Use your unique whistle to identify yourself to another dolphin. Talk to each other in whistles. The sound can even tell them how you are feeling. Once the hunt is over, go back to a smaller pod with new friends.

Ocean mammals

Masters of the sea, ocean mammals include some of the largest animals on the planet. Unlike other sea creatures, marine mammals do not have gills and need to return to the water's surface to breathe. They also give birth to live young, which they nurse with milk they have produced.

I don't believe it
Scientists believe that bowhead whales can live to be more than 200 years old – the longest of any living mammal.

While sleeping, bottlenose dolphins keep one side of their brain awake and alert so that they can watch for predators.

Bearded seal pups are excellent swimmers and can swim and dive to depths of 656 ft (200 m) within hours of being born.

A polar bear has black skin but transparent hairs which reflect light–this is what makes the fur look white.

California sea lions (pictured) like to play and can often be seen body surfing on the waves.

03. Being the social animal you are, hang out with your pals and find the time to play - chase each other, surf the waves, and best of all, blow large bubble rings in the water.

HOLDING ON!
Sea otters wrap kelp, or large seaweed, around themselves to avoid drifting off in the swirling sea currents when they are asleep.

Going the distance

Humpback whales have one of the longest migrations of any mammal. Some populations swim 5,000 miles (8,000 km) from their feeding grounds in the cold waters of the Polar regions to their breeding grounds in the warmer tropical waters.

— Migration routes

Major breeding areas (winter)

Major feeding areas (summer)

Possible nonmigratory permanent residents

Pacific Ocean

Atlantic Ocean

Indian Ocean

Pacific Ocean

① Living and breeding on rocky beaches, this hairy creature hunts for food mostly at night. It can rotate its hind flippers under its body to "walk" on land.

Thick fur traps air to keep it warm.

② This big-eyed mammal has a short snout and very short, coarse fur that helps it swim faster. It uses its keen sight to find and hunt squid in the deep, dark waters under Antarctic pack ice.

Pups are born with dark brown fur.

Broad, white bands on the body are more prominent in males.

③ Living alone or in small groups in the North Pacific and Arctic Oceans, this animal uses the claws on its flippers to move quickly across slippery ice.

Thick, sensitive whiskers are used to find prey and sense predators.

④ Also known as the hook-nosed sea pig, this speedy swimmer can race through the water at speeds of up to 22 mph (35 km/h).

⑤ This Arctic animal gets its name from the long, dense whiskers on its face. It uses them to find clams and invertebrates on the seabed.

Flippers are clapped underwater to communicate.

TEST YOURSELF

STARTER
Northern elephant seal
Gray seal
Atlantic walrus
Leopard seal

CHALLENGER
Hooded seal
Bearded seal
Ribbon seal

GENIUS!
South American fur seal
Ross seal
Galápagos sea lion

Wide gape and sharp teeth help bring down large animals.

6 Named for its spotted coat, this pinniped is a fierce predator that hunts other seals and penguins. It lurks underwater, near floating ice in the Antarctic Ocean, ready to ambush its prey as they dive.

Up to 35½ in (90 cm) long, the ivory tusks are used to climb onto ice.

7 Also called *el lobo marino* in Spanish, meaning "sea wolf," this sociable South American animal makes a sound similar to the barking of a dog.

8 Found in the icy waters around Greenland, this creature feeds on deepwater fish such as halibut and redfish. Males inflate the black nasal cavity on their snout to attract mates.

9 This animal uses its sensitive whiskers to find and eat clams buried in shallow seabeds. Its thick, wrinkled skin turns pink in the Sun as blood flows to the skin's surface and absorbs heat.

Long flippers help it walk on the shore.

Males can also inflate the stretchy red lining of one nostril.

Adults have dark, patchy fur.

10 Weighing up to 6,000 lb (2,700 kg), this large pinniped is named for its elongated, tubelike nose. It is an excellent diver and can swim to depths of 1 mile (1.5 km).

Fin-footed fun

Seals, fur seals, sea lions, and walruses—all mammals that live in and by the sea—are known as pinnipeds. They have finlike flippers, which help them dive to great depths and swim expertly through seas and oceans. Found mostly in cold climates, pinnipeds have thick layers of fat, known as blubber, under their skin to keep them warm.

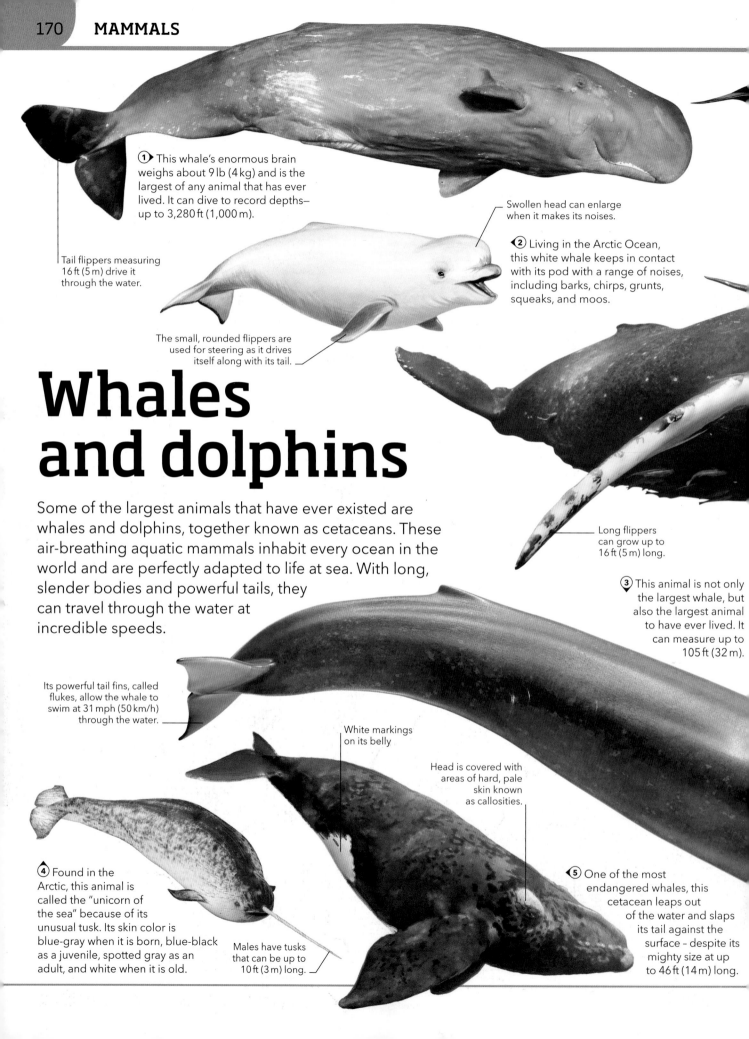

1 This whale's enormous brain weighs about 9 lb (4 kg) and is the largest of any animal that has ever lived. It can dive to record depths— up to 3,280 ft (1,000 m).

Tail flippers measuring 16 ft (5 m) drive it through the water.

Swollen head can enlarge when it makes its noises.

2 Living in the Arctic Ocean, this white whale keeps in contact with its pod with a range of noises, including barks, chirps, grunts, squeaks, and moos.

The small, rounded flippers are used for steering as it drives itself along with its tail.

Whales and dolphins

Some of the largest animals that have ever existed are whales and dolphins, together known as cetaceans. These air-breathing aquatic mammals inhabit every ocean in the world and are perfectly adapted to life at sea. With long, slender bodies and powerful tails, they can travel through the water at incredible speeds.

Long flippers can grow up to 16 ft (5 m) long.

3 This animal is not only the largest whale, but also the largest animal to have ever lived. It can measure up to 105 ft (32 m).

Its powerful tail fins, called flukes, allow the whale to swim at 31 mph (50 km/h) through the water.

White markings on its belly

Head is covered with areas of hard, pale skin known as callosities.

4 Found in the Arctic, this animal is called the "unicorn of the sea" because of its unusual tusk. Its skin color is blue-gray when it is born, blue-black as a juvenile, spotted gray as an adult, and white when it is old.

Males have tusks that can be up to 10 ft (3 m) long.

5 One of the most endangered whales, this cetacean leaps out of the water and slaps its tail against the surface – despite its mighty size at up to 46 ft (14 m) long.

⑥ Growing up to 30 ft (9 m) long, this animal is the smallest baleen whale—whales that feed by filtering small animals from seawater.

Gray "smoky" patches where the black back meets the white belly.

White armbands around flippers

Calves are known to whisper to their mothers.

Large, dorsal fin can be up to 6 ft (1.8 m) long.

⑦ Hunting in large groups called pods, this dolphin is a powerful predator and can even take down great white sharks.

Teeth can grow up to 4 in (10 cm) long.

⑧ At 37 tons this is one of the world's largest and heaviest animals. It likes to sing, often for up to 30 minutes at a time, and its call or "song" can be heard by other whales up to 20 miles (32 km) away.

⑨ Found in the Atlantic, Pacific, and Indian oceans, this cetacean is thought to be one of the most intelligent ocean mammals. It is very playful and will swim and jump alongside boats.

Distinctive pale patch on the side of the body

As a male grows older its bulbous head gets bigger.

⑩ With two long flippers, this cetacean can swim in bursts of up to 20 mph (32 km/h) to chase down prey.

Pleats allow throat to expand to hold a lot of water, from which the whale filters its food.

TEST YOURSELF

STARTER

Humpback whale
Blue whale
Short-beaked common dolphin
Orca

CHALLENGER

Common minke whale
Narwhal
Sperm whale

GENIUS!

North Atlantic right whale
Beluga whale
Long-finned pilot whale

ANSWERS: 1. Sperm whale 2. Beluga whale 3. Blue whale 4. Narwhal 5. North Atlantic right whale 6. Common minke whale 7. Orca 8. Humpback whale 9. Short-beaked common dolphin 10. Long-finned pilot whale

Index

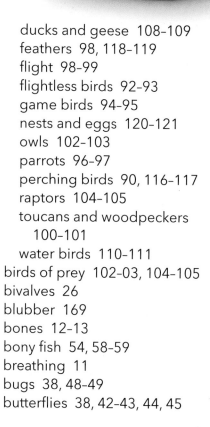

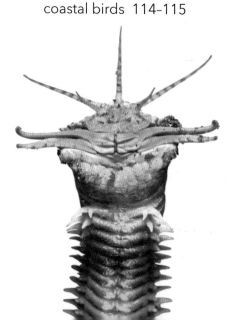

Acknowledgments

The publisher would like to thank the following people with their help with making this book: Ann Baggaley for proofreading; Elizabeth Wise for indexing; Ankita Gupta for editorial assistance; Nishwan Rasool and Vagisha Pushp for picture research; and Priyanka Sharma for the jacket.

Picture Credits

The publisher would like to thank the following for their kind permission to reproduce their photographs:

(Key: a-above; b-below/bottom; c-center; f-far; l-left; r-right; t-top)

123RF.com: Vladislav Gajic 13cla, givaga 152fcl, Eric Isselee 97tr, 175br, Iakov Kalinin 62tl, Werayut Nueathong 39fbr, Theeraphan Satrakom 141cl, Elena Shchipkova / lenor 166clb, Thawat Tanhai 45cr, Ten Theeralerttham / rawangtak 22crb, Dennis van de Water 140tr. **Alamy Stock Photo:** AGAMI Photo Agency / Jari Peltomäki 105ca, Agefotostock / Berndt Fischer 128-129b, agefotostock / C.S. Bettencourt 112tr, Kelvin Aitken / VWPics 56tc, All Canada Photos / Tim Zurowski 5bc, 117bl, All Canada Photos / Wayne Lynch 77clb, David Allemand / Nature Picture Library 145tl, Carl Allen 99crb, Max Allen 152bl, Amar and Isabelle Guillen-Guillen Photo LLC 54cl, Ambling Images 104tr, 114bl, Heather Angel / Natural Visions 159clb, Animal Stock 26-27bc, Art Collection 3 43cl, Arterra Picture Library / Arndt Sven-Erik 106tc, De Meester Johan / Arterra Picture Library 29bl, Avalon.red / Stephen Dalton 48-49cb, Bel 73bl, Brian Bevan 69br, Biosphoto / Frederic Desmette 117crb, Biosphoto / Gerard Soury 57bl, Biosphoto / Steven Kovacs 20clb (Molluscs), Biosphoto / Sylvain Cordier 3tr, 111ca, Sergio Hanquet / Biosphoto 31tl, blickwinkel 39bc (beetle), blickwinkel / A. Hartl 58tl, blickwinkel / B. Trapp 37bl, blickwinkel / Hauke 143cr, blickwinkel / Hecker 155c, blickwinkel / Hecker / Sauer 24cl, blickwinkel / M. Woike 111b, blickwinkel / McPHOTO / A. Schauhuber 41tr, blickwinkel / McPhoto / KFU 147tr, blickwinkel / McPHOTO / LOV 86-87t, blickwinkel / McPHOTO / PUM 91br, blickwinkel / S. Gerth 100br, blickwinkel / Schmidbauer 160-161bc, blickwinkel / Teigler 26cb, Blickwinkel / Trapp 68br, Blue Planet Archive 24-25b, Blue Planet Archive SKO 22tc, Rick & Nora Bowers 114tc, Penny Boyd 162bl, Buiten-Beeld / Daniele Occhiato 99ca, Buiten-Beeld / Jelger Herder 69cla, 71tr, Rich Bunce 73tr, Carlos Villoch - MagicSea.com 62clb, Nigel Cattlin 49c, 49cb, cbpix 27tr, Jenna Chamberlain 80tl, David Chapman 158crb, Helmut Corneli 10-11, 22bc, 34b, Andrew Darrington 46bc, Dave Watts 150bl, David Tipling Photo Library 73tl, 98-99t, DeGe Photo 143tc, E.R. Degginger 64-65, Dembinsky Photo Associates / Skip Moody 105tl, 130tr, Design Pics Inc / Thomas C. Kline, Jr. 59br, Martin Dohrn / Nature Picture Library 142-143b, Andrew DuBois 85crb, Holger Ehlers 93bl, Kevin Elsby 113tl, ephotocorp / Hrishikesh Karandikar 67tr, ephotocorp / Zeeshan Mirza 51crb, David Fleetham 31ca, 33cra, Tim Fleming 134cl, FLPA 72cr, Fotograferen.net 55cra, Lincoln Fowler 133cra, georgesanker.com 149tr, Robert German 14tl, Bernhardt Reiner / Prisma by Dukas Presseagentur GmbH 162-163tc, Jane Gould 56tl, Bill Gozansky 94bc, 163tc, Ken Griffiths 80-81b, Nathan Guttridge 105bl, Steve Hamblin 43tr, Andy Harmer 44-45b, Frank Hecker 56br, 159cla, Chicurel Arnaud / hemis.fr 60ca, Jared Hobbs / All Canada Photos 147tl, Doug Horrigan 80cl, Sean Hunter 152tl, Scott Hurd 112bl, Image Professionals GmbH / Konrad Wothe 96cl, Image Source / Alexander Semenov 25ca, imageBROKER / Christian Hütter 105tc, imageBROKER / Gerry Pearce 127cr, imageBROKER / Marko König 96tl, imageBROKER / Norbert Probst 63tl, J.W.Alker / imageBROKER 31cr, Joe McDonald / Steve Bloom Images 3tl, 125bl, 145tr, Rebecca Jackrel 94tc, Jon Arnold Images Ltd 93tl, Juniors Bildarchiv GmbH 156tl, 174b, Juniors Bildarchiv GmbH / F259 76cl, Juniors Bildarchiv GmbH / F309 97crb, Dave Keightley 101ca, Rolf Kopfle 94bl, Steven Kovacs / Biosphoto 26tl, Ivan Kuzmin 147br, Emmanuel Lattes 39fcla, William Leaman 91tc, Alex Mustard / Nature Picture Library 168c, Jeff Rotman / Nature Picture Library 61bl, Life on white 111cra, Doug Lindstrand / Design Pics Inc 149c, Lazydays Liz 121bl, Colin Marshall 58clb, Tim Mason 112cb, Nobuo Matsumura 62cla, 119cla, Chris Mattison / Nature Picture Library 10clb, mauritius images GmbH / Ronald Wittek 127tr, Robert McGouey / Wildlife 160bl, McPhoto / Rolf Mueller 153cra, Anthony Mercieca / Dembinsky Photo Associates 103cla, Stephen Miller 152cl, Olivier Miniato / Biosphoto 39cb, Richard Mittleman / Gon2Foto 167cr, Jeff Mondragon 55br, National Geographic Image Collection / Brian J. Skerry 78-79b, Natural History Museum, London 49crb, Nature Photographers Ltd / Paul R. Sterry 54tl, Nature Picture Library 17tc, 25cla, 58cb, 72-73b, 158clb, Nature Picture Library / Andrew Walmsley 139tr, Nature Picture Library / Anup Shah 134bl, Nature Picture Library / Guy Edwardes 68tl, Nature Picture Library / John Abbott 47tl, Nature Picture Library / Konrad Wothe 40cr, Nature Picture Library / Lucas Bustamante 41br, Nature Picture Library / Mark Payne-Gill 72tl, Nature Picture Library / Michael D. Kern 50tr, Nature Picture Library / Pete Oxford 56-57c, Nature Picture Library / Rolf Nussbaumer 68cr, S C Bisserot / Nature Photographers Ltd 146br, Naturepix 92c, Andrey Nekrasov 20cl, 23c, 33bl, Pete Niesen 32bl, NOAA 31clb, Paulo Oliveira 57tc, 59tr, 59bl, P&F Photography 86-87b, Papilio / Robert Pickett 35bl, 50crb, Petographer 80clb, Toni Pfaffenbauer / imageBROKER 142tr, Pixels of Nature 51tr, Premaphotos 50tc, George Reszeter 91cb, Bryan Reynolds 48clb, Robertharding / Louise Murray 134tl, William Robinson 117br, Rolf Nussbaumer Photography / Stefan Huwiler 96br, Rolf Nussbaumer Photography / Thomas Marent 48l, Scenics & Science 34cla, Malcolm Schuyl 46bl, Science History Images 128tr, Science Photo Library 44t, Scubazoo 11cr, Scubazoo / RGB Ventures / SuperStock 3clb, 27cla, Martin Shields 50l, Anton Sorokin 46tl, Inga Spence 154cb, Paul R. Sterry / Nature Photographers Ltd 28tc, Steve Bloom Images 125bc, Beth Swanson 62-63b, tbkmedia.de 114cla, Tierfotoagentur / T. Harbig 121br, Genevieve Vallee 92ca, Chris Wallace 115c, WaterFrame_dpr 60cr, WaterFrame_fur 20clb, 23bl, 60tc, 60cl, Michael Weber / imageBROKER 144bl, WENN Rights Ltd 67br, WILDLIFE GmbH 62tr, 94cra, 169cr, 172tr, Tony Wu / Nature Picture Library 170-171c, Konrad Zelazowski 121cra, Zoonar GmbH / Pavlo Vakhrushev 58c, ZUMA Press, Inc. 163ca. **Ardea:** imagebroker.com / Juergen & Chri 150cl, Augusto Leandro Stanzani 166-167, Joanna Van Gruisen 161ca. **Dorling Kindersley:** Thomas Marent 42tl, Thomas Marent 43cla, Thomas Marent 43br, Chris Mattison Nature Photographics 78c, Andrew Beckett (Illustration Ltd) 110br, 117tr, 127ftr, 135tc, 137tl (branch), 137bc, 145cr, Geoff Brightling / Booth Museum of Natural History 12-13c, Chris Gomersall Photography 94cb, Cotswold Wildlife Park & Gardens, Oxfordshire, UK 135tr, Philip Dowell / Natural History Museum, London 12cra, 121tl, Terry Goss 57cb, Colin Keates / Natural History Museum 12cb, 12b, 12-13b, Twan Leenders 71c, 78tl, 83tl, Richard Leeney / Whipsnade Zoo 96-97t, Natural History Museum, London 2tr, 2ftl, 42clb, 42bl, 43c, 133bc, Natural History Museum, London / Harry Taylor 35tc, Linda Pitkin 32tc, Lynette Schimming 39br, Kim Taylor / Natural History Museum, London 121tc, 121cla (chicks), 121ca, Wildlife Heritage Foundation, Kent, UK 150tc, Jerry Young 26cr, 43bl, 69clb, 77tc, 77tr, 78cb, 86c, 146clb, 156tr. **Dreamstime.com:** Agami Photo Agency 132tl, Agdbeukhof 47tl, 110cb, Akvals 32tl, Allexxandar 62cra (background), Almir1968 55cra (Underwater), 55crb, Greg Amptman / Thediver123 57tr, Amwu 36bl, 78bl, 79tl, 79cr, 96c, Annaav 145crb, Artushfoto 145br, Andrew Astbury 124fbr, Auris 20clb (grass), Avslt71 99cr, Rinus Baak 118tl, Tatiana Belova 59ca, Ben 95clb, Birdiegal717 107ca, Karel Bittner 33tr, Lukas Blazek 126bl, 131b, 153cla, Bobhilscher 76bl, David Burke 154cr, Barbara Burns 38fcra, Steve Byland 106bl, Jeremy Campbell 29bc, Cathywithers 132tc, Vladimir Cech 145clb, Cherdchai Chaivimol 47b, Mun Lok Chan 101tc, Chernetskaya 147ftr, Coconutdreams 29crb, Shubhrojyoti Datta 97tc, Davthy 164c, Digitalimagined 47br, 47b (black ants), Dimarik16 141tr, Miloslav Doubrava 90clb, Dreamzdesigner 14br, Ecophoto 139br, Elantsev 14ftl, EPhotocorp 37tr, 82br, Dirk Ercken 67cr, Rudolf Ernst 93cra, 109ca, Farinoza 70clb, 138tr, Feathercollector 144c, Nicolas Fernandez 26bl, Phil Feyerabend 108tl, Gerald Robert Fischer 25tr, FlorianAndronache 110tl, Svetlana Foote 14tr, 124bl, Forest71 37cb, Fotomicar 161cr, Domiciano Pablo Romero Franco 39ca, Aleksandr Frolov 164tl, Charles Gibson 165ca, Godruma 11bc, Golfxx 62cra, Natalia Golovina 93b, Joaquin Gonzalez Gomez 104bl, Grotmarsel 26cra, Andrey Gudkov 121cb, Gillian Hardy 4tl, 137cl, Alexander Hasenkampf 47c, 48cra, David Havel 139tc, 175tl, Hel080808 99br, Vasyl Helevachuk 118cr, Moose Henderson 104cla, 113cr, Henrikhl 37cr, Mikael Holgersson 84br, Hvat10 157c, Isselee 4-5bc, 5tc, 35ca, 35cl, 36-37t, 38cra, 39cra, 60cra, 68clb, 68bl, 69tr, 71bc, 86-87ca, 92br, 96bl, 97bc, 119c, 121cla, 129cla, 131ca, 153br, 173cra, Roman Ivaschenko 38ca, Izanbar 61cr, 166cl, Jayone1981 155crb, Vladislav Jirousek 137tc, 149bc, Jnjhuz 130cl, John braid / Johnbraid 4-5tc, 43cb, Jens Stolt / Jpsdk 42tr, Jsanerkin 157bl, Karin59 160cl, Katephotographer 83br, Kengriffiths6 82clb, Klaphat 140cla, Klomsky 85tr, KMWphotography 141bl, Tetiana Kolubai 48c, Tetiana Kovalenko 139tc (Leaves), Denis Kovshutin 36crb, Matthijs Kuijpers 4cra, 70bl, 78tr, 79cla, Dalia Kvedaraite 135bc, Kwiktor 92l, Thomas Langlands 140cb, Leerobin 81crb, Tom Linster / Flinster007 148tl, Chris Lorenz 107bl, Lucaar 145c, Lunamarina 132-133bc, Luna Vandoorne Vallejo / Lunavandoorne 125br, Lars S. Madsen 41c, Suvit Maka 15tc, Aliaksandr Mazurkevich 124tl, Mealmeaw 125fbl, Martin Mecnarowski 105br, Sander Meertins 102tc, Katho Menden 2c, 157tl, Joseph Mercier 14ftr, Mikelane45 5cla, 90cl, 105cb, 130clb, 131tl, Simonas Minkevičius 108tc, Mirecca 59c, Natakuzmina 35clb, Luca Nichetti 138bl, Duncan Noakes 2ca, 40crb, Andy Nowack 20cla, Office2005 84clb, Okea 68cr (water), Matthew Omojola 4br, 42br, Jason Ondreicka 71clb, Mohamed Osama 124cl (Underwater), Chansom Pantip 136tc (branch), Yuri Parmenov Yuri Parmenov 120bc, 120br, Pecak 136tl, Martin Pelanek 66bc, 101br, Phassa 158cr, Photobee 49cla, Picstudio 115br, Picture.jacker 124bc, Pincarel 39bc, Pipa100 24tl, Verabutr Piriyanontana 76clb, Planetfelicity 58b, Elena Podolnaya 58crb, Alain Poirot 138-139c, Stu Porter 162ca, Ondřej Prosický 10clb (bird), 103ca, 104clb, Denisa Prouzová 141ca, Daniel Prudek 161tr, Penchan Pumila 63crb, Subin Pumsom 141crb, Pzaxe 4bc, 41cr, Constantinoff Richard 107br, Jasper Rimpau 27br, David Roberts 168-169c, Jonas Rönnbro 108cr, Stefan Rotter 112tc, Juan Carlos Martínez Salvadores 107clb, Sarah2 37clb, Scheriton 140cl, Juergen Schonnop 10cla, Seadam 33crb, Visa Sergeiev 155clb, Alexander Shalamov 113cl, Peter Shaw 112cla, Kai Shen 108bl, Skalapendra 11br, Slowmotiongli 66bl, 96crb, 104tc, 116clb, 134cra, 136tc, 153tr, 166tl, Smellme 157clb, Aleksey Solodov 32tr, Stillwords 155tl, John Stocker 160ca, Stripe1964 29cr, Stuartan 108br, Stubblefieldphoto 63br, Kasira Suda 41ca, I Wayan Sumatika 39cl, Sergey Taran 84cra, Piyapong Thongdumhyu 24tr, Dimitar Tzankov 114cl, Sergey Uryadnikov 156b, Vaeenma 146tl, Vicki Vale 29cb, Veronika Verenin 106bc, Victortyakht 117tl, Vasiliy Vishnevskiy 130c, Viter8 27cr, 40ca, 78cra, Natalia Volkova 127b, Vrabelpeter1 85ca, Aekkaphum Warawiang 76crb, Sarayut Watchasit 5ca, 22clb, Yael Weiss 125cra, Buddee Wiangngorn 28b, Ivonne Wierink 15tl, Wiltding 15cr (background), Wirestock 76clb (Turtles), William Wise 129c, Marcin Wojciechowski 160tr, Cezary Wojtkowski 161tl, Wrangel 58tr, 157br, 159cr, Vladimir Melnik / Zanskar 169tr, Zhbampton 40cl. **FLPA:** BIA / Alan Murphy 100tl, Dembinsky Photo Ass. 128bl, Kevin Elsby 163cr, Michel Gunther 163b, Daniel Heuclin / Biosphoto 143br. **Getty Images:** 500px / BP Chua 108-109t, 500px / Martin Anderson 36cla, 500Px Plus / Jelly Fish 18-19, 500Px Plus / Tony Beck 95tr, AFP / Yasuyoshi Chiba 16-17b, AGAMI stock 109c, Enrique Aguirre Aves 169b, Sjoerd Bosch 115t, Corbis Documentary / Arthur Morris 110bl, Corbis Unreleased / Frans Lemmens 126tl, Gerald Corsi 152-153bc, Cultura / Rodrigo Friscione 58-59c, De Agostini / DEA / C.Dani / I. Jeske 134bc, DigiPub 5tr, 29tl, Georgette Douwma 61br, Troup Dresser 39c, Rohit Kushwah / EyeEm 124-125, Gamma-Rapho / Dave Watts 116cl, Gamma-Rapho / Sylvain Cordier 45tr, H Photos / EyeEm 155cla, James Hager 133tl, Ken Kiefer 2 56ca, Raimund Linke 2fcla, 137c, Alexander Safonov / Barcroft Media 60b, Moment / © Juan Carlos Vindas 119tc, Moment / Amith Nag Photography 8-9, Moment / Artur Carvalho 88-89, Moment / Floridapfe from S.Korea Kim in cherl 134-135b, Moment / Joao Paulo Burini 36tr, Moment / Larry Keller, Lititz Pa. 98-99b, Moment / Stan Tekiela Author / Naturalist / Wildlife Photographer 129tc, Andrey Nekrasov 30cl, 59tl, Photodisc / Ken Usami 34tr, Photographer's Choice RF / Barry Kusuma 3br, 81t, Photographer's Choice RF / Ronald Wittek 119bc, RooM / shikheigoh 76-77c, Sumiko Scott 38b, Paul Starosta 158c, The Image Bank / Martin Harvey 122-123, Universal Images Group / Education Images / David Tipling 95crb, Vicki Jauron, Babylon and Beyond Photography 151tr, Nimit Virdi / 500px 151b, Westend61 102tl. **Getty Images / iStock:** aaprophoto 130br, adogslifephoto 134c, aedkais 107tl, AGAMI stock 119clb, al_la 165tr, anan kkml 150cra, Andreygudkov 150c, Antagain 97ca, 97cra, barbaraaaa 119crb, BirdImages 106br, blueringmedia 67tl, Neil Bowman 93ca, brentawp 4tc, 116tc, cellistka 82-83c, 174tl, chaiyon021 135cra, chris2766 102-103t, clark42 125cr, Catherine Withers-Clarke 118tr, Cloebudgie 158bl, CraigRJD 144br, cynoclub 97clb, DarrenMower 33tl, DavidByronKeener 108cb, davidevison 142ftl, Denja1 54cla, Dgwildlife 116tl, DKart 138cl, drakuliren 117c, E+ / 33karen33 115cl, E+ / animatedfunk 49tc, E+ / DieterMeyrl 2tl, 94ca, E+ / Gannet77 164cl, E+ / KeithSzafranski 2cla, 114tr, E+ / Zocha_K 106cl, eastriverstudio 159ca, EcoPic 142tl, ePhotocorp 101clb, Farinosa 81tr, GlobalP 4cra (fox), 48ca, 71tl, 81cla, 84-85c, 129tr, 144tr, Goddard_Photography 162cr, hugy 155tr, italiansight 10c, JackVandenHeuvel 110-111t, JensenChua 92-93t, JimGallagher 136tr, jkauffeld 17br, Joesboy 47crb, johnandersonphoto 23bc, 23br, kajornyot 106cb, Kaphoto 47clb, KenCanning 144-145c, kojihirano 46cla, Zoran Kolundzija 106cr, Mark Kostich 83tr, leonello 124cla (Platypus), Enrique Ramos Lopez 100-101t, marrio31 61clb, MattCuda 119cra, mauribo 115tl, mdesigner125 103br, MichaelStubblefield 61tr, namibelephant 159tc, Enrico Pescantini 128tc, PetlinDmitry 82tr, PhanuwatNandee 95br, alessandro_pinto 165clb, reptiles4all 74-75, 85bl, richcarey 83c, Dwi Septiyana 94br, Simoneemanphotography 133cr, skynesher 154clb, slowmotiongli 131tr, StockPhotoAstur 101tr, Sundry Photography 84ca, taviphoto 161cl, Lillian Tveit 137br, USO 90-91b, Martin Voeller 70cb, wholden 165tl, Albert Wright 118ca, Michael Zeigler 166cla. **naturepl.com:** Ingo Arndt 28cb, Emanuele Biggi 47ca, Bernard Castelein 2clb, 111clb, 138bc, Nigel Cattlin 26tc, Jordi Chias 169tl, 170t, Stephen Dalton 36tl, 36br, Sue Daly 30bl, Richard Du Toit 158tl, 161br, Michael Durham 63clb, Guy Edwardes 102bl, 114tl, David Fleetham 57ca, Michael & Patricia Fogden 66clb, 69tl, Steve Gettle 110crb, Edwin Giesbers 148br, Doug Gimesy 132cl, Chris Gomersall / 2020VISION 47cl, Melvin Grey 68tr, Shane Gross 30cr, Erlend Haarberg 115cb, Brent Hedges 135cb, Daniel Heuclin 82-83bc, 138tl, Klein & Hubert 131cra, Denis-Huot 165b, Alex Hyde 50cra, 51cb, Ernie Janes 5ftr, 47tr, Hilary Jeffkins 73crb, Chien Lee 129cb, Will Burrard-Lucas 130tl, Malleefowl 95bc, Roy Mangersnes 121cb, Bence Mate 102cb, MYN / Gil Wizen 36ca, MYN / Javier Aznar 82cl, MYN / Lily Kumpe 40tc, Piotr Naskrecki 146c, Nature Production 38cra (Bombardier), 54-55b, Greg Oakley 102br, Gary Bell / Oceanwide 31c, Pete Oxford 85c, David Pattyn 116tr, Doug Perrine 55cr, Loic Poidevin 20-21c, 116bl, Premaphotos 51clb, Andy Rouse 136bl, Tui De Roy 1cb, 115bl, 167cra, Phil Savoie 38cla, 38cl, 38cr, 38br, Scotland: The Big Picture 91cl, 113tr, Roland Seitre 130cr, Anup Shah 136cr, Shattil & Rozinski 152tr, Igor Shpilenok 159bl, Kim Taylor 10tl, 22br, 69cra, Andy Trowbridge 97cla, Markus Varesvuo 109tc, Colin Varndell 159tl, Marion Vollborn / BIA 109br, Dave Watts 91tl, Tony Wu 21br. **Reuters:** Stringer 39tr. **Robert Harding Picture Library:** Tom Campbell 33cla, Patrick Frischknecht 153cr. **Science Photo Library:** Dr. John Brackenbury 48tr, Dante Fenolio 73cla, Leonard Rue Enterprises 155bl, Merlintuttle.org 146tr, Gilles Mermet 28tl, Piotr Naskrecki / Nature Picture Library 154br, B. G Thomson 147cra. **Shutterstock.com:** aaltair 25tl, Kurit afshen 66-67c, Stacey Ann Alberts 120, Aleksei Alekhin 20bl, ananth-tp 10cl, AP / Frank Glaw 77cra, Aumsama 148tr, Bildagentur Zoonar GmbH 70tr, bluecrayola 107tc, Mark Brandon 39clb, 40tr, Vladimir Cech 149crb, Jesus Cobaleda 41bl, Richard Constantinoff 118cl, Curioso. Photography 132-133tc, emperorcosar 149tl, Federico.Crovetto 72ca, Sanit Fuangnakhon 40b, GraphicRN 152cb, Nikolas Gregor 51bl, ichywong 157tr, imageBROKER.com 162br, Eric Isselee 86tl, 132clb, Matt Jeppson 77br, Vladislav T. Jirousek 151cb, JonathanC Photography 151cla, Breck P. Kent 26-27tc, Jean Landry 109cla, Fabio Maffei 66br, Fauzan Maududdin 16-17ca, Christian Musat 164r, Serkan Mutan 110tc, Mircea Negulici 108cra, Jesse Nguyen 116-117c, Zaruba Ondrej 135ca, Marieke Peche 51cla, James Marvin Phelps 133br, PhotocechCZ 160cr, Francesco_Ricciardi 24cra, S. Aratrak 159br, sakhorn 84-85t, Shpatak 55tr, Sandra Standbridge 51tl, Rostislav Stefanek 22bl, Marek R. Swadzba 49tr, TCreativeMedia 111tc, unterwegs 26bc, Anton Watman 10bl, Milan Zygmunt 103c. **SuperStock:** Age Fotostock / Colin Marshall 25bc, 172bl, Stephen Belcher / Minden Pictures 15b, BIA / Minden Pictures / Alan Murphy 100bl, Biosphoto 13crb (x3), 154tc, Biosphoto / Ignacio Yufera 100cla, D. Parer & E. Parer-Cook / Minden Pictures 140br, Suzi Eszterhas / Minden Pictures 140ca, Michael & Patricia Fogden / Minden Pictures 14cr, CORDIER Sylvain / Hemis 168tl, Imagemore 41tl, juniors@wildlife Bildagentur G / Juniors 148bl, Hiroya Minakuchi / Minden Pictures 132b, Minden Pictures / Stephen Belcher 35br, Minden Pictures 46r, 52-53, Minden Pictures / Buiten-beeld / Henny Brandsma 111cb, Minden Pictures / Michael & Patricia Fogden 128tl, Minden Pictures / Mitsuhiko Imamori 45ca, Minden Pictures / Stephen Dalton 50bc, NHPA 127bc, 139cb, Pacific Stock - Design Pics / Dave Fleetham 20ca, Pantheon / Elizabeth Bomford 72tr, Steve Downeranth / Pantheon 30br, Kevin Schafer / Minden Pictures 124cl, Michael Durham / Minden Pictures 124fr, Tui De Roy / Minden Pictures 168tr, Universal Images Group 31br, ZSSD / Minden Pictures 163cl. **Unsplash:** Luke Tanis / @saluken 142ftr

All other images © Dorling Kindersley
For further information see: www.dkimages.com

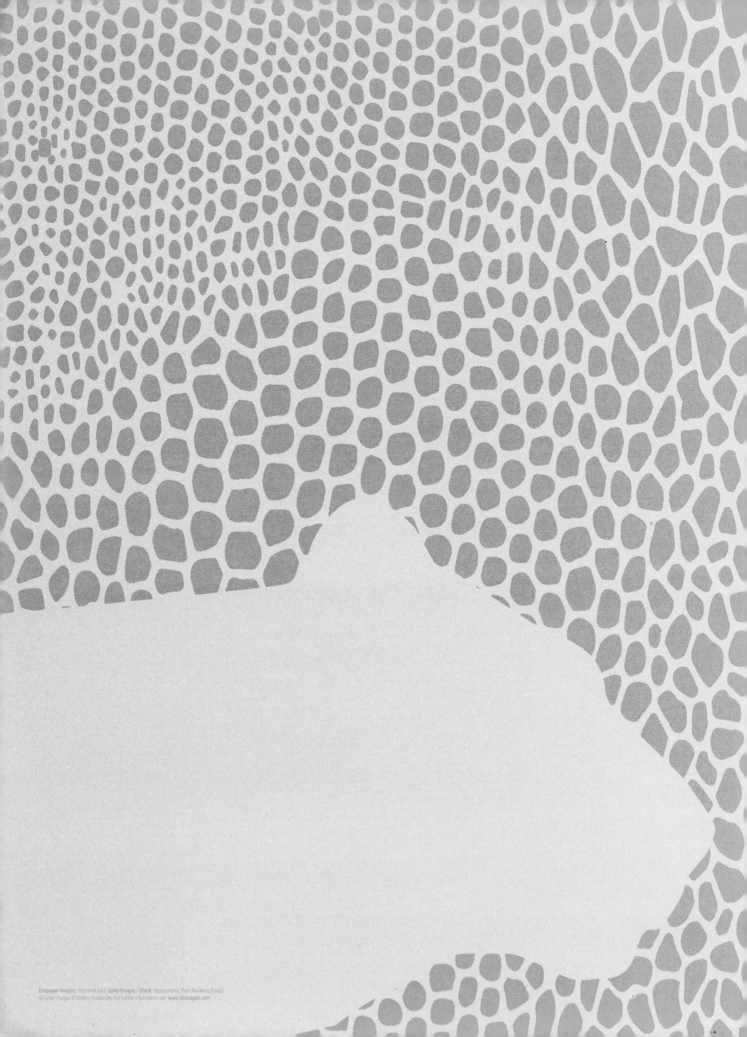